CANAL HOUSE
COOKING

Canal House
No. 6 Coryell Street
Lambertville, NJ 08530
thecanalhouse.com

ISBN 978-0-615-34070-8

Printed in U.S.A.

Book design by Canal House, a group of artists who collaborate on design projects.
This book was designed by Melissa Hamilton, Christopher Hirsheimer & Teresa Hopkins.
Favorite Wines by Julie Sproesser.
Authors' photo by Teresa Hopkins.
Edited by Margo True.
Copyedited by Valerie Saint-Rossy.

CANAL HOUSE
COOKING

Volume N° 3

Hamilton & Hirsheimer

Christopher and Melissa in the Canal House kitchen

Welcome to Canal House—our studio, workshop, dining room, office, kitchen, and atelier devoted to good ideas and good work relating to the world of food. We write, photograph, design, and paint, but in our hearts we both think of ourselves as cooks first.

Our loft studio is in an old red brick warehouse. A beautiful lazy canal runs alongside the building. We have a simple galley kitchen. Two small apartment-size stoves sit snugly side by side against a white tiled wall. We have a dishwasher, but prefer to hand wash the dishes so we can look out of the tall window next to the sink and see the ducks swimming in the canal or watch the raindrops splashing into the water.

And every day we cook. Starting in the morning we tell each other what we made for dinner the night before. Midday, we stop our work, set the table simply with paper napkins, and have lunch. We cook seasonally because that's what makes sense. So it came naturally to write down what we cook. The recipes in our books are what we make for ourselves and our families all year long. If you cook your way through a few, you'll see that who we are comes right through in the pages: that we are crazy for tomatoes in summer, make braises and stews all fall, and turn oranges into marmalade in winter.

Canal House Cooking is home cooking by home cooks for home cooks. We use ingredients found in most markets. All the recipes are easy to prepare for the novice and experienced cook alike. We want to share them with you as fellow cooks along with our love of food and all its rituals. The everyday practice of simple cooking and the enjoyment of eating are two of the greatest pleasures in life.

CHRISTOPHER HIRSHEIMER served as food and design editor for *Metropolitan Home* magazine, and was one of the founders of *Saveur* magazine, where she was executive editor. She is a writer and a photographer.

MELISSA HAMILTON cofounded the restaurant Hamilton's Grill Room in Lambertville, New Jersey, where she served as executive chef. She worked at *Martha Stewart Living*, *Cook's Illustrated*, and at *Saveur* as the food editor.

Trees leaf out in early spring along the Delaware & Raritan Canal that flows past Canal House

Waiting for Spring

WE ARE DEAD IN THE MIDDLE OF WINTER. The air is full of snow all day but only an inch accumulates. It's cold when we arrive at the studio in the morning and we work with our hats on until the wood fire warms up the place. It is so quiet now with the French doors shut tight—no noise floats up from the street below. We hibernate, sitting at our desks wrapped in sweaters and scarves. As we write and cook, we listen over and over (as if teenagers) to a CD mix that a friend made for the studio. We warm ourselves with big bowls of watercress soup for breakfast.

We instigate teatime. Every afternoon at three-thirty the sun sinks behind the hill, and suddenly the room feels chilly again, so we shake flames out of the embers and throw another log on the fire. When the kettle whistles we brew cups of milky tea and serve ourselves buttered wheat crackers with fat Medjool dates. So what if we put on a couple pounds over the winter—who will notice under all these clothes. Sitting in the waning light, we talk about what we will plant in our spring gardens.

Even though it's cold, we build up our appetites, taking walks with children, dogs, and friends, crunching down the towpath through the snow. The canal has frozen and it looks like we could skate all the way up to Frenchtown, fifteen miles away. You can take the cold when you know there is a pot of something bubbling away on the stove at home.

The farmstand market on the edge of town has closed for the season, so there is no sliding in on the way home at the end of the day to grab something for dinner. We can't rely on vegetables we don't have this time of year! We are both eating out of our pantries—dried beans and lots of pasta. Now we're in tomato-wilderness time, so we pull out our summer stash from deep in the freezer. It's the ant and the grasshopper fable, and preserving last summer's bounty is paying off big time. We stir pesto into penne. Spread herb butters on fish or roasted chicken. And oven-roasted tomatoes, tomato sauce, and rich tomato paste find their way into everything.

A new indoor farmers' market has opened on the weekend in a vacant building just a few miles up the river. There are fresh eggs (thirteen varieties of heirloom chickens are still laying) and amazing cheesemakers—Jonathan and Nina White of Bobolink Dairy & Bakeyard, with piles of medieval-looking loaves of levain and slabs of raw cow's milk cheeses that astound us with their gutsy, primitive styles and flavors. The line is longest at Metropolitan Seafood. The fishmongers arrive with coolers full of sparkling fresh fish—calamari, skate, grey sole, diver scallops from Nantucket, cod—all caught from cold winter waters and now packed in shaved ice. Fish is the new weekend flavor and takes the place of the Sunday Roast on our families' menus. We buy some for the studio too, and fold cod into potatoes and fry fish cakes for lunch.

When we fancy a ham for a friend's birthday dinner, it's time to check out a butcher that comes highly recommended. So we are off to Illg's Meats, seventeen miles away over hill and dale on country roads that used to wind through rich farmland, but now development encroaches on the fields. We see the sign for Illg's Meats, "The Best of the Wurst" and pull off the road and down a long lane. The market is in a low building in the middle of a classic farmyard with a big stone barn, and a large stone house with white ruffled curtains in every window. Inside, the shop is immaculate. The meat cases are full of sausages of every kind, beautifully displayed. To us this looks better than the jewelry case at Tiffany's. Hams are on sale so we buy a beauty—a twenty-pounder. When we get it back to the studio, it's too big for our roasting pan so we bake it long and slow in a big blue speckled enamelware lobster pot. It works out great, so easy to transport—handles and a lid. There's half a ham left over so we pass it back and forth between our neighbors and ourselves till the damn thing is gone.

Then one day it is warm enough to leave the doors open. And we notice the sky is staying light later. We wait for the sure sign of spring, the day the canal is stocked with trout. Soon men will come on their lunch hour and stand on the bank casting their lines into the water, hoping for a catch. After school, boys barely in their teens come to fish, and we watch them posturing in the watery spring sunlight, smoking cigarettes and swearing at each other.

Here in the Northeast, even after spring arrives it will still be a long while before the markets will be bustling. But there will be asparagus, sorrel, spring onions, chives, rhubarb, and more. There will be plenty for us to cook!

Christopher & Melissa

It's Always Five O'Clock Somewhere

MARTINI
makes 2

Our dry vermouth stays fresh in the fridge. The gin lives in the cupboard. The soft cucumber and rose flavors of Hendrick's Gin suit our taste. As to how dry a dry martini should be, it seems to us that it should be just wet enough to keep it from tasting like an icy cold glass of rubbing alcohol, no? It's a very fine line.

4 ounces gin   Cocktail olives
½ ounce or less dry vermouth

Put gin and dry vermouth into an ice cube–filled cocktail shaker. Stir gently. Strain into two ice-cold martini glasses. Garnish each with a few toothpick-speared olives. Drink responsibly.

HALF AND HALF
makes 2

There was a time when a martini was equal parts gin to dry vermouth, stirred, not shaken. When we have the taste for a gin martini but aren't feeling macho enough for a dry one, we fix ourselves one of these wet lovelies.

2 ounces gin   2 dashes bitters
2 ounces dry vermouth   2 strips lemon zest

Put gin, dry vermouth, and bitters into an ice cube–filled cocktail shaker. Stir gently. Strain into two ice-cold stemmed glasses. Garnish each with a twist.

MARGARITA

Colman Andrews, our drinks guru, always uses tequila made of 100 percent agave, Cointreau rather than Triple Sec, and little Key or thin-skinned limes for his grown-up, tart version of this cocktail.

Squeeze the juice of 2 thin-skinned limes into a cocktail shaker filled with ice cubes. Rub the rims of two martini glasses with one of the cut lime halves. Pour some fine sea salt into a saucer and roll the wet rims in the salt. Pour 3 ounces premium tequila and 1–2 ounces Cointreau into the shaker, cover with the lid, and shake until the margarita is very cold and well mixed. Strain into the salted glasses and serve.—*makes 2*

While we like to start with a cocktail, when we get into the real business of eating dinner, we drink wine. We asked a few serious wine drinkers what they are drinking right now. If you can't locate their exact suggestions, ask your local shop for something similar to take a chance on.

MARIO BATALI needs no introduction. He owns many of our favorite restaurants, owns very famous orange clogs, and drinks a lot of Italian wine.

Morellino di Scansano "I Perazzi," La Mozza, Italy, 2006
I love the wine "I Perazzi" by my farm in Maremma, Toscana. It has a juicy mouthfeel, cherry flavors, and an incredible sense of place that brings me back to Toscana with every glass I drink. This simple wine tastes more like a wine born in the fields of vines and not in the lab or the winery. I am drinking my reds a little cooler these days, right at cellar temp, 55°–60°. And in the same sense I am drinking my whites a little warmer, say just below cellar temp 48°–52°.

Bastianich Friulano, Italy, 2007
I drink more white than red and often drink it as an aperitivo and then continue along the same vinous path with dinner, so I am always looking for a wine that tells me where it is from and that is not so manipulated or blended. Joe Bastianich's Friulano has become the benchmark for all winemakers in Friuli, and his wine is fresh and light, with hints of citrus and crisp green apple acidity.

RANDAL BRESKI spends half the year in Paris and half in San Francisco. He and his partner David Tanis are the coolest cats we know and we always want to know what they are drinking.

Château de la Presle, Touraine, France, 2007
This white is delicious, simple, and refreshing. It has none of the strident sauvignon blanc qualities often found in new-world wines. It has a gentle acidity and fresh fruit, making it good for an apéritif or a first course.

Domaine de Pierredon, Côtes du Rhône, France, 2007
A terrific, pretty, sturdy red. With warm, pleasing, dark aromas and cherry-berry fruit in the glass—once it has been open a bit—it lacks overwhelming tannins. Great with all the stewy things, like braised duck legs and beef cheeks cooked in red wine and oxtails. Yummy.

DARRELL CORTI owns the renowned Corti Brothers Fine Wine & Gourmet Foods Italian Grocery Store in Sacramento. He has flawless taste in all things.

Dingač, Plavac, Croatia, 2007
This plavac from Croatia's Peljesac peninsula is good, not black in color, and it has a light, spicy aroma with a delicious, almost cranberrylike flavor that points up its refreshing acidity and moderate alcohol.

Corti Brothers H.P.O., Oregon, 2008
Corti Brothers has an exclusive on this early muscat wine, which is a cultivar invented at UC Davis by Professor Harold Olmo, whose initials form the wine's name. It is fragrant, low alcohol (6%), and has residual sugar that is bolstered by nice acidity. It is a delicious wine for sipping.

MANI DAWES owns Tía Pol, a tapas and wine bar in New York City, and Tinto Fino, a great Spanish wine shop on the city's Lower East Side.

Can Feixes Negre, Spain, 2006
A unique, limited production from Penedès in Cataluña, this blend of cabernet sauvignon, merlot, and tempranillo, with a kick of petit verdot is the antidote to big winter reds. Soft tannins with a touch of earth, herbs, and restrained berry fruit—it's warm but still bright and versatile.

Valdesil "Val de Sil", Spain, 2008
Godello was on the verge of extinction, but this native Galician varietal has had a bit of a renaissance. Valdesil's sees no oak, but has a depth that comes straight from the grape and the hillside slate soils. With ripe, luscious pear and musky grassiness, coupled with a racy acidity, it makes an unexpectedly rich winter white.

GABRIELLE HAMILTON is a writer and the chef-owner of Prune restaurant in New York City. She always knows what's delicious.

Weingut Stein Blauschiefer Riesling Trocken, Germany, 2008
I like that this wine is delicious, but also that I can drink a lot of it without getting drunk, have a bottle open in the refrigerator for days and it doesn't go bad, and even drink a little glass of it in the afternoon and it just feels like a beverage and not a narcotic.

Domaine de Durban, Beaumes de Venise, France, 2005
I think I've bottomed out on giant reds for good. I eternally want medium-bodied reds, especially in the winter, and this one is friendly without food but still plenty tannic and structured. I've been drinking mightily delicious Italians for a long time now, but this wine reminded me of what the elegant French do effortlessly, how they get that very elegance into the bottle—even in their rustic stuff, and, still pack smoke, tar, barnyard, and stone walls into even a minor vineyard's bottling. It makes it seem like the Italians are shouting and wearing bright orange sweaters while the French are just speaking in quiet tones in navy blue sweaters, letting their genius speak for itself.

DAN MELIA is our German wine authority. He represents Mosel Wine Merchant, a collection of Mosel growers specializing in delicious, dry Rieslings.

Domaine Léon Barral Faugères, France, 2006
In some capacity it screams winter wine, but I actually first drank this Faugères in the summer, so I feel comfortable recommending it for the bridge season that is winter/spring. It has all the power, fruit, and warmth to soothe when that is what the temperature requires, but it remains a lovely wine with just enough bite to make you hopeful, come April, that you can fire up the grill and cook something with a bit of char that will bite back.

Peter Lauer, Ayler Kupp "Senior" Fass 6 Riesling, Germany, 2008
I am currently obsessed with this wine. It is fresh, chiseled, and depending on how much time you give it in the glass or in the fridge, either bright and lean or round and relatively powerful, or some delicious amalgam thereof. The whites I've been drinking lately are all Riesling, all from Germany's Mosel Valley, mostly in the dry or off-dry style, rather than the higher-residual-sugar style with which most Americans are familiar. If it has been a while since you tried one out, or if you live deathly in fear of sweetness (you shouldn't), try a Riesling labeled trocken (dry) or

maybe feinherb (off-dry), and I bet you'll be surprised at how different it is from what you have had in your mind's eye.

MICHAEL STEINBERGER writes the wine column for *Slate*. He also recently wrote *Au Revoir to All That: Food, Wine, and the End of France*, published by Bloomsbury, 2009.

Pierre Moncuit Brut NV Champagne, France

The great economist John Maynard Keynes said his one regret in life was that he didn't drink enough Champagne. That's a mistake I'm determined to avoid, and Moncuit is helping me avoid it. Moncuit is a small, excellent producer, and its non-vintage Champagne, made entirely of chardonnay and bursting with lemon and chalk flavors, is an elegant, thoroughly refreshing bubbly that I could happily drink every day.

Caves Cooperatives de Donnas Rosso, Italy, 2005

This red is essentially a baby Barolo and I became smitten with it last year. From the Vallée d'Aoste region of Italy, it is composed mainly of picotendro, which is the local name for the nebbiolo grape. It is a warm, complex, thoroughly lip-smacking wine that is affordable enough to be habit-forming.

PARDIS STITT owns and operates Highlands Bar and Grill, Bottega, Café Bottega, and Chez Fonfon restaurants in Birmingham, Alabama, with her husband Frank Stitt.

Bailly Lapierre Crémant de Bourgogne Brut Rosé NV, France

This is a beautiful bubbly that I love turning people on to—made of pinot noir, it reminds me of strawberries and it is such a value you can drink it every day!

Terredora di Paolo Fiano di Avellino, Italy, 2008

I really enjoy the white wines of Campania and the Terredora di Paolo is one of my favorites. Dry, but with an almondlike quality, this wine has a richness that works well as an aperitivo or with food. Think seafood, tomato, fennel, olives, and olive oil.

Charles Joguet Chinon, France

Chinon makes me happy, especially from Joguet. These reds of the Loire Valley have a lightness and are not weighed down with oak—juicy-fruit without the sweetness. A classic by the glass or carafe at Parisian bistros and cafés, it makes me imagine being at Le Select (or Chez Fonfon in Birmingham)!

working up an appetite

Melissa, Margo True, and Niloufer Ichaporia King in Niloufer's San Francisco kitchen

NILOUFER'S SUCKY PEAS

Niloufer Ichaporia King includes this recipe in her wonderful book *My Bombay Kitchen* (University of California Press, 2007). The idea is to pull the peas out of the pods with your teeth, just as you would eat an artichoke leaf. The charred bits of the pod and the salt sticks to your lips, flavoring the tender peas.

Pour a little extra-virgin olive oil into a large cast iron pan. Wipe the pan out with a paper towel, leaving the thinnest film of oil. Heat the pan over high heat. When it's very hot, add 1 pound organic English peas in their pods in a single layer, turning them with a spatula until they turn from bright green to a blistery blackened olive color. Work in batches. Transfer to a plate, sprinkle with Maldon or any other coarse, flaky salt and serve right away.—*serves 2–6*

MARTINI-SOAKED STUFFED OLIVES

Sometimes the best part about drinking a martini is eating the olive. Why not serve them up front and center instead of wading through all that alcohol just to get to the olive? We serve these as an hors d'oeuvre at cocktail hour.

Put 1 cup gin and ¼ cup dry vermouth into a quart container or bowl. Add 2 drained 5- to 8-ounce jars large green stuffed cocktail olives and gently stir. Cover and refrigerate the olives until they've had a chance to macerate and become well chilled, 1–2 hours. Serve the olives cold with the martini juices in a wide dish, and with toothpicks for spearing.

CRAB SALAD WITH CLUB CRACKERS

When we have the freshest lump crabmeat available to us, we do little more than dress it with a bit of mayonnaise and lemon juice. When we have a hankering for crab and can only find the pasteurized tubs of it, we dress it like this and serve it with a fresh box of Club crackers.

Put 1 small finely chopped onion, 1 finely diced inner rib of celery, 1 finely chopped scallion, 2 tablespoons capers, ½ cup mayonnaise, 1 small handful chopped fresh dill, and juice of 1 lemon into a medium bowl and mix well. Gently fold in 1 pound jumbo lump crabmeat. Add a little more lemon juice if you want and season with salt and pepper. Serve with Club crackers. —*makes 2½ cups*

CHICKEN LIVER PÂTÉ

Don't hold back on the butter—it is the very thing that makes this delicate pâté so velvety smooth. This is a version of the pâté served at The Ranch House in Ojai, California.

Melt 3 tablespoons butter (preferably Kerrygold Irish butter) in a large sauté pan. Add 1 bunch chopped, trimmed scallions and cook until softened, about 3 minutes. Add 12 ounces chicken livers and cook until just cooked but still pink inside, 5–7 minutes. Remove from heat, add 1 teaspoon salt, 1 teaspoon ground allspice, and 1 generous tablespoon Dijon mustard. Purée in a food processor, adding 3 more tablespoons butter as you blend, until very smooth. Add a splash of Cognac, if you like. Transfer to a well-oiled mold or small bowls, cover with plastic wrap and refrigerate until firm, about 8 hours. Unmold and serve with toasts or crackers sprinkled with minced chives.—*makes 2 cups*

LIMAS & PRESERVED LEMON

Frozen limas work as well as fresh for this recipe. Or if you like, substitute cooked lentils or white beans.

Purée 2 cups cooked lima beans along with 1 clove minced garlic, 2–4 tablespoons really good olive oil, salt to taste, and lots of ground black pepper. Serve with toast drizzled with olive oil and garnished with chopped preserved lemon rind.—*makes about 2 cups*

BLUE CHEESE AND WATERCRESS MASH

Make a double batch of this savory spread to keep in your fridge—it will be like money in the bank. Spread it on crackers or little toasts and serve them as hors d'oeuvres or with a big bowl of soup.

Mash together 1 bunch watercress, stems trimmed, leaves finely chopped, 1 bunch finely chopped chives, ¼ pound blue cheese, and 2 tablespoons softened butter together in a small bowl. Season with salt and pepper. (The cheese may be salty enough, so taste before adding salt.) Spread on little toasts or crackers and garnish with fresh watercress, if you like.—*serves 4*

LEMON AND SEA SALT FOCACCIA
makes four 8-inch rounds

Every bite of this rustic, salty, and intensely lemony focaccia is a mouthful of delicious tart flavors. Use a really good buttery olive oil to tame it.

FOR THE DOUGH

1 envelope (2¼ teaspoons)
  active dry yeast
6 tablespoons really good
  extra-virgin olive oil
4 cups bread flour, plus more
  for kneading
2 teaspoons salt

TO ASSEMBLE

Really good extra-virgin olive oil
Leaves of 2–4 branches fresh
  rosemary, chopped
2 lemons, washed and very thinly
  sliced into rounds
Coarse sea salt

For the dough, dissolve the yeast in ½ cup warm water in a medium bowl. Stir in 1¼ cups water and 2 tablespoons of the olive oil.

Pulse the flour and salt together in the bowl of a food processor. Add the yeast mixture and process until a rough ball of dough forms, 1 minute. Briefly knead dough on a floured surface until smooth. Shape dough into a ball. Put 2 tablespoons of the oil into a large bowl. Roll dough around in bowl until coated with oil. Cover the bowl with plastic wrap and let the dough rise in a warm spot until it has doubled in size, about 2 hours.

Pour a thin film of oil into each of four 8-inch round cake pans. Quarter the dough and put one piece into each pan. Using your fingertips, spread dough out in each pan. The dough is elastic and will resist stretching. Let it relax for 5 minutes or so after you've stretched it as far as it will go. Eventually, it will cooperate and fill the pan.

Preheat the oven to 450°. Cover the pans with damp dishcloths and let the dough rest until it has swollen in the pans a bit, 30–60 minutes.

Uncover the pans. Sprinkle dough with the rosemary. Using your fingertips, poke dimples into the dough in each pan, then liberally drizzle with oil so it pools in the hollows. Arrange just the thinnest rounds of lemon on top, drizzle with more oil, and sprinkle with sea salt. We like ours salty. Bake the focaccia until golden brown, 20–30 minutes. Drizzle with more oil when you pull the focaccia from the oven. Serve cut into wedges.

Teatime

MARMALADE
makes 3 pints or 6 half pints

"Here is the recipe I inherited from Mum. It is the best marmalade I have ever eaten and so very, very worth the making of lots. Mum had a knack for barely setting her preserves and always asked in a most concerned voice if she had cooked them enough. We could never answer except with eagerly nodding heads as our mouths were stuffed with good things dripping with these lovely preserves".—*Jeremy Lee, chef of Blue Print Café, London*

3 pounds (about 5 oranges)
  Seville or sour oranges
2 lemons

2 grapefruits
Demerara sugar

Cut stem and blossom ends off the oranges. Using a sharp paring knife, remove the peel along with only a little of the pith. Thinly slice the peels and put them into a large bowl. Halve and juice the oranges. Add the juice to the bowl with the sliced orange rinds. Roughly cut up the juiced oranges, and transfer them along with any seeds to a piece of doubled muslin large enough to tie up into a pouch.

Grate rind from the lemons and grapefruits and add it to the orange slices. Juice the fruit, add the juice to the orange slices, and add the chopped, juiced fruit to the muslin. Gather up the muslin into a tight pouch and tie with kitchen string.

Add the pouch along with 12 cups water to the orange slices and juice. Set aside to soak overnight or for up to 24 hours.

Transfer the oranges, juice, and pouch of pips and pulp to a pot. Bring to a boil over medium-high heat, reduce heat to low, cover, and simmer until the peel is tender, about 1½ hours. The liquid will have reduced by about a third. Remove the bag from the pot, and set aside until cool enough to handle. Squeeze the pouch and release any juices back into the pot. Discard the pouch.

Measure the amount of oranges and juice then return all to the pot. Add an equal amount of sugar. Bring the marmalade to a boil over medium-high to high heat, stirring constantly, until the sugar has dissolved. Continue boiling rapidly without stirring until it reaches its setting point, 220°. Remove from heat and allow to cool for about 10 minutes. Gently stir to disperse any scum (it is only air bubbles). Fill hot sterilized jars with the marmalade to ¼ inch from the top. Seal with hot sterilized lids and rings. Allow to cool undisturbed for 24 hours.

CANDIED ORANGE PEEL
makes about 3 dozen

We like fat, meaty strips of candied orange peel instead of the thin sticks you often see. The bitter tender rind just underneath the crunchy sugar coating makes a nice little something to have in the middle of the afternoon with a cup of tea or an espresso. To fancy them up, we sometimes dip the tips in melted semi- or bittersweet chocolate—then they're really like eating a confection.

3 navel oranges, skins scrubbed under warm water to remove any wax coating
3 cups sugar

I vanilla bean
I star anise or small branch fresh rosemary

Working with 1 orange at a time, slice the ends off the fruit, just exposing the flesh. Set the orange on one of the cut ends and slice off the rind and white pith together in nice fat wide swaths, exposing the flesh. Try to keep from cutting into the flesh as much as you can. Trim off any flesh clinging to the white pith.

Put the peels into a heavy, medium pot of cold water and bring to a boil. Drain. Return the peels to the same pot with fresh cold water and bring to a boil again. Drain.

Put 2 cups of the sugar and 3 cups water into the same pot. Cover and bring to a boil over medium-high heat. When the sugar has dissolved, after about 1 minute, add the orange peels, vanilla bean, and star anise or rosemary.

Reduce the heat to low and simmer, partially covered, until the peels are soft and the syrup is a thick glaze (a little thicker than the consistency of corn syrup), about 2 hours.

Lay the peels out on a cooling rack so they don't touch each other and let them dry like this until they are tacky. Dredge a few pieces at a time in the remaining 1 cup sugar. Lay them out again on the cooling rack to dry completely. Store in an airtight container.

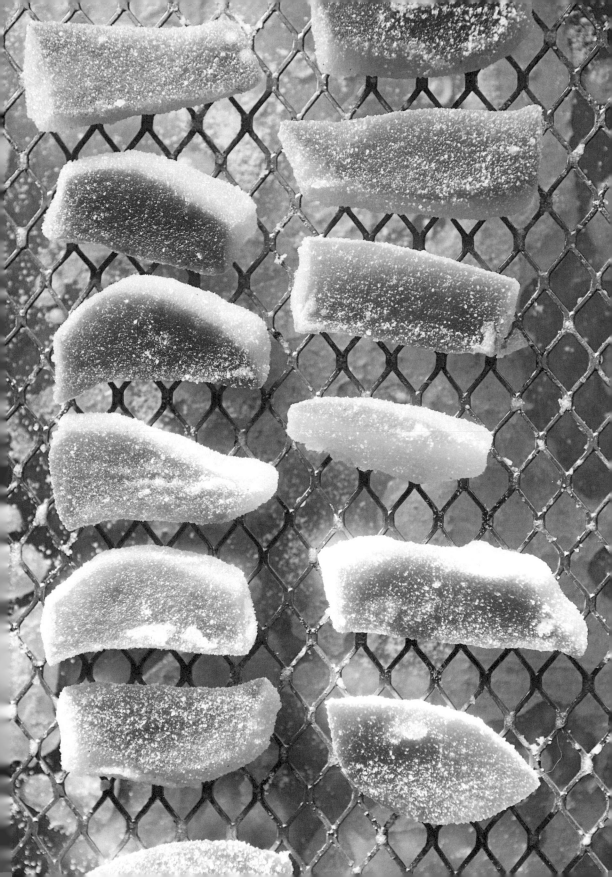

DATES AND BUTTERED WHEAT CRACKERS

We were feeling a bit peckish, but too lazy to go to the store. We put the kettle on and rummaged around in the pantry to see if perhaps there was a cookie or two hiding out behind a jar of pickles. No luck! But on the top shelf, a box of Carr's Whole Wheat Crackers was sitting right next to a package of Medjool dates. As the tea brewed, we generously buttered the crackers with a good smear of Irish butter and pitted the dates. We ate and sipped by the fire, content to be right where we were.

HAM THAT LOOKS LIKE BACON
makes 24 little sandwiches

These old-fashioned ribbon sandwiches, with their stripes of white bread and pink ham look like—yes, that's right—slices of bacon.

⅔ cup Major Grey's mango chutney
12 tablespoons softened butter
Salt and pepper

12 slices thin white sandwich bread
8 slices ham

Stir together the chutney and 8 tablespoons of the butter in a small bowl. Season with salt and pepper. Lay out the slices of bread on a clean surface and spread each slice with the chutney butter, making sure you spread right to the edge. Make a triple-decker sandwich with the bread and ham like this: top one of the slices of bread with a slice of ham, then with a slice of bread, then with another slice of ham, then with a slice of bread, buttered side down. Repeat the sandwich-making process with the remaining bread and ham to make 4 triple-decker sandwiches in all.

Cut off the crusts and any overhanging ham, squaring off each sandwich. (The sandwiches can be made ahead up to this point. Keep them covered and refrigerated until you're ready to cook them.)

Melt the remaining 4 tablespoons of butter in a large skillet over medium-low heat. Add the sandwiches and cook on both sides until golden brown, 3–5 minutes per side. Remove the sandwiches from the skillet and slice into thirds then cut each piece in half to make 24 little sandwiches. Serve warm, garnished with minced fresh chives or parsley, if you like.

salads

HEARTS OF PALM AND BLOOD ORANGE SALAD
serves 4

Choose hearts of palm packed in glass—the canned ones always taste tinny. Red-fleshed blood oranges come into markets in January; however, navel or other "orange" oranges make fine substitutes.

2 blood oranges
½ teaspoon Dijon mustard
I tablespoon fresh lemon juice
Salt and pepper

3—4 tablespoons really good
 extra-virgin olive oil
I jar (14.8 ounces) hearts of palm,
 drained and halved lengthwise
Small head frisée lettuce

Working with one orange at a time, slice the ends off the fruit. Set the orange on one of the cut ends and slice off the rind and white pith, exposing the flesh. Working over a bowl to catch any juice, slice between each fruit segment, cutting it away from the membrane and let the segments and juice fall into the bowl. Squeeze any juice from the spent fruit into the bowl.

Stir the mustard and lemon juice together in a wide bowl. Add a bit of salt and some pepper, then stir in the blood orange juices from the first bowl. Whisk in the olive oil. Taste the vinaigrette and season to your liking. Add the hearts of palm to the bowl, gently turning them in the vinaigrette while keeping them intact.

Arrange the frisée and hearts of palm in a wide serving bowl or dish. Place the orange segments on top of the hearts of palm. Pour the vinaigrette over the salad and drizzle a little more olive oil over all.

CHOPPED RAW ASPARAGUS AND PEA SALAD
serves 4

This is the perfect use for those spindly thin asparagus!

¼ cup grated pecorino romano
¼ cup really good extra-virgin olive oil
Pepper
2 bunches pencil-thin fresh asparagus, trimmed and sliced crosswise

I cup shucked peas, blanched
4 scallions, finely chopped
4—8 large butterhead lettuce leaves
8 pieces cooked bacon, finely chopped
I handful fresh mint leaves, chopped

Put the cheese into a big bowl, add ¼ cup hot water, and stir until the cheese melts. Whisk in the olive oil and season with pepper. Add the asparagus, peas,

continued

and scallions and toss well. Adjust the seasonings. Arrange the lettuce leaves on individual plates or on a serving platter. Spoon the salad onto the leaves, then scatter the bacon and mint on top.

MOCK CAESAR
serves 2–4

Caesar salads can be such a disappointment—floppy dark green outer leaves tossed with thick, sweet, creamy parmesan dressing. The poor maligned Caesar! We have to confess, we too mess with the authentic version of this classic—omitting, among other things, the coddled egg and the Worcestershire sauce. We crush garlicky croutons and sprinkle them over the salad at the end. It's our mock Caesar—but it's anything but a mockery of the original.

I clove garlic, chopped
3–4 anchovy fillets, chopped
Salt and pepper
I teaspoon Dijon mustard
Juice of I lemon

5–6 tablespoons extra-virgin olive oil
½ cup grated parmigiano-reggiano
2–4 hearts romaine lettuce
½ cup crushed garlicky croutons, optional

Crush the garlic, anchovies, a good pinch of salt and grinding of pepper, and the mustard into a paste with a mortar and pestle or with the tines of a fork in a medium bowl. Stir in half the lemon juice, then the olive oil, and half of the grated parmigiano-reggiano. Adjust the seasonings.

Depending on the thickness of the hearts of lettuce, halve or quarter them lengthwise. Arrange the lettuce on a serving platter or on individual plates. Spoon the dressing over the leaves and sprinkle the crushed croutons, if using, and the remaining parmigiano on top. Drizzle with a little extra olive oil.

CRUNCHY WINTER SALAD
serves 4

We make this salad in the dead of winter when we're craving something bright, cold, and crunchy with our meal. Even when it seems like there is

continued

hardly a thing to choose from in the vegetable section of the grocery store, most of these veggies show up in fine shape year-round.

Rind from ¼ preserved lemon, finely chopped

2–3 anchovy fillets, chopped

Salt and pepper

Juice of 1 lemon

½ cup really good extra-virgin olive oil

4–5 ribs celery with leaves, sliced

1 fennel bulb, quartered and sliced

1 bunch radishes, sliced

½ head radicchio, sliced

1 Belgian endive, thickly sliced

3–4 scallions, sliced

1 handful fresh mint leaves, chopped

1 handful fresh parsley leaves, chopped

Put the preserved lemon, anchovies, a pinch of salt and lots of pepper, and the lemon juice into a large salad bowl. Stir in the olive oil. Add the celery, fennel, radishes, radicchio, endive, scallions, mint, and parsley. Cover and refrigerate the salad for an hour. Toss and adjust seasonings.

RADICCHIO WITH HARD-BOILED EGG & CRISP PANCETTA
serves 4

This pleasantly bitter salad is our winter (and, let's face it, much more flavorful) version of the iceberg wedge.

2 scallions, white and green parts separated and finely sliced

2 tablespoons balsamic vinegar

1 tablespoon wine vinegar

Salt and coarsely ground pepper

5–6 tablespoons really good extra-virgin olive oil

2 heads radicchio, quartered lengthwise

2 hard-boiled eggs, peeled and chopped

½ cup crisp-fried diced pancetta or thick-sliced bacon

1 small handful fresh parsley leaves, chopped

Put the sliced white part of the scallions into a small bowl. Add the vinegars and a good pinch of salt and grinding of pepper. Stir in the olive oil.

Set the radicchio wedges on individual plates or on a serving platter. Spoon the vinaigrette over the radicchio and garnish each wedge with chopped egg, pancetta, the scallion greens, and chopped parsley.

FRENCH ONION SOUP
serves 6–8

This is quite a miraculous soup—the miracle of the onion. It tastes like it has simmered on the stove for days, but you can make a big pot in a couple of hours.

FOR THE SOUP
3 tablespoons extra-virgin olive oil
3 pounds yellow onions, thinly sliced
2 cloves garlic, sliced
2 bay leaves
Freshly ground black pepper
2 tablespoons flour
1 large tablespoon Dijon mustard

1 bottle white wine, or red wine
   if you prefer
4–6 cups chicken stock
Salt

FOR THE TOASTS
Butter
6–24 slices baguette
½ pound Gruyère, thinly sliced

For the soup, heat the oil in a large, heavy pot over medium heat. Add the onions, garlic, and bay leaves and cook, stirring often, until the onions are soft and brown, about 20 minutes.

Season with pepper and stir in the flour. Cook for a few minutes to remove the raw flour taste. Stir in the mustard. Add the wine and stir to mix everything together. Increase the heat to medium-high and cook until the soup comes to a simmer, about 10 minutes. Add 4 cups of the stock and, when the soup comes to a vigorous simmer, reduce the heat to medium-low. Gently simmer the soup until it has developed a rich flavor and has thickened slightly, 45–60 minutes. Add more stock if needed. Season to taste with salt and pepper.

For the toasts, butter both sides of the bread slices then toast them on both sides until lightly browned in a preheated broiler. Top the toasted bread slices with the Gruyère and return to the broiler until the cheese is bubbly and golden.

Meanwhile, ladle the soup into bowls. Float some of the cheese toasts on top of each.

BEET SOUP CANAL HOUSE STYLE
serves 4–6

When our IT advisor and dear friend Echo Hopkins had a very unfortunate accident that fractured her jaw, we knew what the girl needed—the healing power of our puréed vegetable soups. We made batches of our four favorite flavors to coax her into taking a little liquid nourishment. It is the simplest recipe in the world. For something fancier you can dress it up just before serving with a dollop of sour cream, chopped chives, or crumbled bacon, or anything else you have a yen for. This story has a happy ending—Echo recovered her beautiful smile. We think it was the soup! —— CH

4 beets (2 pounds)
4 tablespoons butter
I large yellow onion, chopped
Salt and pepper

I large russet potato, peeled
  and chopped
Rind from ¼ preserved lemon
  (or more if you like)
4 cups chicken stock

Preheat the oven to 375°. Wrap each beet in aluminum foil and bake until tender, 1–2 hours. Unwrap the beets and when they are cool enough to handle, peel off their skins. Coarsely chop the beets and set aside.

Melt the butter in a large heavy pot over medium heat. Add the onions and cook, stirring occasionally, until soft but not browned, about 10 minutes. Season with salt and pepper. Add the potatoes, beets, preserved lemon, and 3 cups of the chicken stock. Cover and cook until all the vegetables are very soft, about 1 hour.

Allow the soup to cool slightly. Working in small batches, purée the soup in a blender or food processor until very smooth. (We have had the hot soup blow the lid off a blender! But cooling the soup and working in small batches will avoid this problem.) Add more stock if the soup is too thick. Season with salt and pepper and serve hot or cold, garnished or plain.

CARROT SOUP: Substitute 2 pounds peeled carrots for the roasted beets and add a big piece of fresh ginger. Remove and discard the ginger before puréeing.

POTATO LEEK: Substitute 4 trimmed, washed, chopped leeks for the roasted beets, and use 2 large russet potatoes instead of one.

BUTTERNUT SQUASH: Substitute 1–2 pounds peeled, seeded butternut squash for the roasted beets. Sweeten the soup with a few tablespoons maple syrup.

Christopher making soup for Echo

WATERCRESS SOUP
(or, how to cure what ails you)
serves 4–6

On my first visit home from my freshman year in college, I stayed with my father, who had recently moved to a little house on a beautiful wooded road. Homesick, I laid low and slept a lot. I remember my father was always offering me something to eat, something he was preparing, some meal, always preparing a meal. Watercress grew in the stream beside the house. I'd wander down there and watch it. Tenacious white roots attached to slippery rocks held all but the delicate green leaves of the cress below the water, the leaves rested flat on the stream's surface. After a while I'd wade into the cold water and gather big clumps of the peppery cress to bring back to the house for my father to use for a salad or a watercress soup. It wasn't until last winter that I remembered how that soup (and those meals) had restored me. I had cabin fever that I needed to shake, so I forced myself to take a walk, asked my husband to come along, and off we went up the wooded creek road near our house. Everything was brown and white and frozen hard to the ground, the black creek cutting through the scene. Then we spotted a green patch in the dark wetness. Something vibrant green and alive. Watercress, growing there in the trickling water. It made me so happy. As did the soup I made, a simple one like this, similar to my father's, made from the cress we'd gathered that day. —— MH

2 bunches watercress, stems
  and leaves separated
8 cups rich chicken stock
2 tablespoons butter
I tablespoon olive oil

I medium onion, finely chopped
I waxy potato, peeled and diced
I handful fresh parsley leaves,
  chopped
Salt and pepper

Gently simmer watercress stems in the stock in a medium pot for 15–20 minutes. Melt butter and oil in another pot over medium-low heat. Add onions and cook until soft. Add the potatoes. Strain the stock into the pot with the potatoes; discard stems. Cook over medium heat until potatoes are tender, 10–15 minutes.

Finely chop the watercress leaves and add them to the stock along with the parsley. Season with salt and pepper. Simmer the soup for just a few minutes, then remove it from the heat. Serve the soup garnished with a knob of butter, a spoonful of heavy cream, or a dollop of crème fraîche or sour cream.

AT YOUR VEGETABLES

by
Patricia Curtan

ew things make me happier than making chicken stock and setting in a supply of olive oil and wine; it gives me a feeling of security, like having a stack of firewood on the porch when the weather turns cold. I find great pleasure in thinking about the pantry, taking mental inventory of the basic stores, and planning for their restocking. With the essentials in the house, my food-obsessed daydreaming shifts to the few key ingredients that inspire a meal.

Early in the day I start thinking about what might be for lunch. (I mostly work at home so the kitchen is conveniently close.) Last night's extra serving of roast chicken would make tasty chicken salad sandwiches, or would it be better in a soup or with pasta? Is there enough for two? It's a little chilly today. There's chicken stock in the freezer, maybe a quick soup with the leeks and some greens. Salad? A head of escarole for lunch or dinner? No, better for dinner, with an anchovy dressing, garlic croutons, and parmesan cheese. That leads to thoughts of dinner. Is there something delicious waiting to be cooked, or do I need to shop?

While it is endlessly interesting to imagine the possibilities of what to cook and how to cook it, I welcome the constraints of having a modest number of fresh ingredients on hand. I subscribe to the "less is more" philosophy. I would rather have just a few really delicious ingredients in the refrigerator than an abundance of choices that I know I won't get to for days. That means shopping more frequently, but I don't mind, especially when it's a farmers' market day and there is the prospect of finding something special—like Annabelle's beans.

Annabelle Lenderink, in Bolinas, California, is an extraordinary farmer. She has got "it", the green thumb or whatever that talent is (and, of course, the intelligence and hard work ethic). Everything she grows is bursting with flavor; her vegetables, alone or in combination, easily become the most exciting thing on the plate. She specializes in a few crops: Italian varieties of chicory and greens; fennel and thin yellow beans; nettles, herbs, and wild arugula; and squashes and pumpkins. But it's her fresh shell beans that arouse passions. She grows cannellini, coco negro, coco bianco, cranberry, and the sublime, tender, pale green flageolet beans.

To go home with a bag of her beans (or two or three, let's be honest) is to know you have a treasure in store. The beans will be delicious cooked any number of ways: with sausages or roast pork; a minestrone soup with tomatoes and pasta; a ragoût with sautéed wild mushrooms and garlic; or my favorite, all by themselves. This is especially satisfying as a private thing: freshly-shelled beans simmered until tender in salted water with a few herbs and a splash of olive oil, spooned into a bowl and seasoned with coarse salt, crushed black pepper, and a generous drizzle of the best olive oil in the house. Along with toasted crusty bread and a glass of red wine, the simple bowl of beans is a divine meal. I couldn't ask for more.

STEWY ROASTED ROOT VEGETABLES
serves 4

Roasted root vegetables have such deep, earthy flavors that you can make this delicious stew and never miss the meat!

4 tablespoons olive oil
1 large yellow onion, sliced
2 cloves garlic, sliced
4–6 large shallots, peeled
Salt and pepper

1 small butternut squash, peeled, seeded, and cut into pieces
4 carrots, peeled and cut into pieces
4 parsnips, peeled and cut into pieces
2 cups white wine
3 small bay leaves

Preheat the oven to 350°. Heat 2 tablespoons of the oil with the onions, garlic, and shallots in a large skillet over medium heat. Season with salt and pepper. Cook until just soft and lightly browned, about 15 minutes. Arrange the squash, carrots, and parsnips in a large baking pan. Scatter the onions, garlic, and shallots and any pan juices around the vegetables in the baking pan. Season with salt and pepper. Add the wine and tuck in the bay leaves. Add a drizzle of olive oil and roast until vegetables are tender, about 1 hour. Serve with chopped fresh parsley, if you like.

Put 1 cup French lentils into a small baking dish with a lid. Add 1 bottle white wine and a drizzle of olive oil, cover, and bake at 350° until tender, about 1 hour. Season with salt and pepper. The stew and lentils will be ready at the same time.

CARROTS & BUTTER

Sometimes poor old carrots can languish in the bottom of the vegetable drawer, forgotten. Perhaps there is a perception that they take a long time to cook, but not so. Melissa likes to peel small, thin carrots then leave them whole, while I love little carrot coins. Cut them into any shape that you like. But no matter how you slice them, if you cook them this way your carrots will be bathed in a buttery glaze. —— CH

Cut 4–8 peeled carrots into coins or any shape you like. Put them into a pot, add about 1 cup of water, stock, or wine, season with salt, and add a few table-spoons good butter. Gently simmer the vegetables until the water evaporates, the carrots are tender, and have absorbed the butter. Season with salt and pepper and some chopped fresh mint, if you like.—*serves 4*

ROASTED SPRING ONIONS
serves 4–6

Spring onions (not to be mistaken with green onions or scallions) make
their appearance at the markets beginning in April. We see them with more
frequency now than just a couple of years ago, and with a growing season
that extends all the way into August. Spring onions are Mr. Universe to the
96-lb. weakling scallion. You'll see them sold in bunches, the thick green
stalks gathered together just above the naked white or blush purple (usually
fat) bulbs. These deliciously mild onions are immature storage onions, and
due to their increased popularity, farmers are staggering their plantings,
pulling the young bulbs from the ground throughout the spring and on
into the summer to extend the season.

6–8 whole spring onions,   Salt and pepper
  long green stems attached   Balsamic vinegar
Extra-virgin olive oil

Preheat the oven to 500°. Arrange the onions in a single layer in a heavy roasting pan. Douse them with some olive oil and generously season them with salt
and pepper.

Roast the onions until deeply browned all over, about 20 minutes. Reduce the
oven temperature to 250° and continue roasting them until the bulbs are tender, 10–15 minutes longer. Remove the onions from the oven and drizzle them
with a couple small spoonfuls of balsamic vinegar, turning them in the pan to
coat them with the pan juices. Season with a little more salt. These are equally
delicious served warm from the oven or at room temperature.

RISI E BISI
serves 6

We like to welcome in spring and the arrival of fresh peas as the Venetians do, with this soupy rice and pea dish. Though it resembles risotto, it shouldn't be as thick as that—rather it should be loose enough that you need a spoon to get every last bit from your bowl.

2 tablespoons extra-virgin olive oil
4 tablespoons butter
1 onion, finely chopped
2 cups shucked peas
Salt

6 cups hot chicken or vegetable stock
1½ cups carnaroli, arborio, or other Italian short-grain rice
½ cup freshly grated parmigiano-reggiano
Pepper

Heat the olive oil and 2 tablespoons of the butter together in a heavy medium pot over medium heat. Add the onions and cook until soft and golden, 5–10 minutes. Add the peas and season with salt. Cook for a minute or two, then add 1 cup of the hot stock.

Cover the pot, reduce the heat to medium-low, and simmer the peas until they begin to soften, about 5 minutes.

Stir in the rice and 4 cups of the remaining hot stock. Cover the pot and adjust the heat to maintain a gentle boil. Cook the rice, stirring occasionally, until just tender, about 20 minutes.

Remove the pot from the heat and moisten the rice and peas with the remaining 1 cup of stock. Stir in the remaining 2 tablespoons of butter and half of the parmigiano-reggiano. Season with salt, if it needs it, and with pepper. Serve sprinkled with the remaining cheese.

gone fishing

Melissa, and Stacy Rose with "lunch" on the canal bridge in front of Canal House

TROUT WITH PANCETTA
(the day Snooky and Little Doc came to lunch)
serves 4

"Hey, ladies! Hey, ladies! Would you like some fish?"

On a spring morning these words blew in through the open windows of our second story studio. On the bank of the canal below, Stacy Rose patiently fished for brook trout. We had exchanged waves as we watched him come every morning for a couple of weeks, unpacking his gear, baiting his poles, keeping his catch in a big white plastic bucket. Not bothering to take off her apron, Melissa ran down to retrieve his gift—four shining fish. Naturally we invited him, along with our neighbor (Melissa's father), for lunch. No introductions were necessary. The two men had known each other since childhood, having both grown up in Lambertville, where they ran around town together in their younger days. Back then, Stacy went by the nickname "Snooky" (his brother was "Spooky") and Jim Hamilton was "Little Doc" (his father was the town doctor). It was amusing and charming to hear these distinguished gentlemen call each other by their childhood names. We sat and listened to tales of the old days and ate the delicious trout. You never know what rich experiences life will hand you if you are open to giving and receiving. —— CH

12 tablespoons (1½ sticks) softened butter

1 large handful fresh parsley leaves, chopped

6–8 fresh chives, finely chopped

Salt and pepper

4 whole cleaned trout

12–16 very thin slices pancetta

Olive oil

1–2 lemons

Combine the butter, parsley, chives, and some salt and pepper in a small bowl. Divide the butter between the trout, tucking it into the belly cavity. Drape 3–4 slices of pancetta over each fish, overlapping the slices. Refrigerate the trout until the butter is firm.

Preheat the oven to 400°. Drizzle some olive oil into a roasting pan large enough to accommodate the trout in a single layer. Arrange the fish in the pan and drizzle a little more olive oil over the fish. Season with salt and pepper. Roast the fish until the pancetta is crisp (or beginning to) and the trout are cooked through, 15–20 minutes. Serve the trout with pieces of lemon.

STEAMED FISH WITH A BUTTERY SORREL SAUCE
serves 4

A few years ago we each bought ourselves a sorrel plant. It is the star of our home gardens and still going strong—the first to shoot up in the spring (and the last to go to sleep in the fall).

4 fillets fresh white-fleshed fish such as halibut or cod, 6–8 ounces each

3 tablespoons white wine vinegar

3 tablespoons white wine

1 scallion, minced

Salt and pepper

12 tablespoons (1½ sticks) cold Irish butter, cut into pieces

8–12 sorrel leaves, stems trimmed, leaves finely chopped

Steam the fish in a covered steamer basket set over a pot of simmering water over medium heat until just cooked through and the flesh turns opaque.

Gently boil the vinegar, wine, scallions, and a pinch of salt and pepper in a small saucepan over medium heat until there's only about 2 tablespoons of liquid left in the pan. Reduce the heat to low and whisk in the butter, one piece at a time, waiting for each piece to completely melt and be emulsified before adding the next one. Stir the sorrel into the thickened butter sauce at the end. Serve a nice spoonful of the sorrel sauce on top of each piece of fish.

FISH CAKES

We make these either with fresh fish or to use up leftover fish and/or potatoes. Serve them with a good tartar sauce and wedges of lemon on the side.

Sweat 1 finely chopped onion in 2 tablespoons butter in a small skillet over medium-low heat until soft, 5–10 minutes. Transfer them to a medium bowl. Break up 2 boiled, peeled russet potatoes, and 1½ pounds steamed cod or halibut fillets into meaty chunks and add them to the bowl. Gently mix in 1 whole egg, 1 egg yolk, ¼ cup chopped fresh parsley, and ¼ cup panko (adding a little more if the mixture is too moist). Season well with salt and pepper. Shape into 8 fish cakes, then coat each one in more panko.

Melt 6 tablespoons butter with 2 tablespoons olive oil in a large skillet over medium to medium-low heat. Fry the fish cakes, adjusting the heat so they don't burn, until golden brown on each side, 5–7 minutes per side.—*makes 8*

Birds of a Feather

CONFIT OF DUCK LEGS
makes 6

The ancient technique of cooking and preserving duck in its own fat is one we take great pleasure in doing ourselves. And the duck legs themselves (we only confit the whole legs) are exquisite eating—silky-tender and full-flavored. We use them in our cassoulet (see page 72), *bien sûr.* Or we'll brown them in a skillet and serve with braised, sturdy greens or stewy legumes. The duck fat is delicious, too; we pan-fry potatoes in it and serve them with the legs. Making a confit is remarkably easy, and we encourage you to try it if you like duck and have never done it yourself before.

You'll need some duck fat to start off with. Supermarket ducks won't yield enough rendered fat to cover the legs completely. So buy some tubs of duck fat. You can reuse it for making subsequent batches of duck confit. If you can't find whole duck legs easily, buy whole ducks and carve them off the carcass, keeping the drumsticks attached to the thighs. Then cut out the breast meat into nice fat lobes for sautéing—they tend to be lean and dry so don't bother to confit them. There's lots of skin, too. Cut it up, render the fat from it, and add it to your stash. Then make duck stock with the carcass. Quite a remarkable use of duck!

6 whole duck legs

2 tablespoons coarse salt

1 bay leaf

8 cups rendered duck fat

Preheat the oven to 250°. Melt the rendered duck fat in a deep, heavy pot over low heat. Remove the pot from the heat. Slip the duck legs into the warm fat. The legs should be completely submerged. Add the bay leaf to the pot. Transfer the pot to the oven and gently cook the legs until they are very tender, 2½–3 hours.

Transfer the legs, bay leaf, and fat to a deep bowl, crock, or pot, making sure the legs are completely submerged in the fat. Cover and refrigerate the confit of duck for at least 2 days or up to 3 months. The flavor improves with time. Gently pry the legs out of the fat as needed, re-covering any legs you're not using with the cold fat. The fat can be reused to make more confit of duck. The jelly at the bottom of the pot is delicious and you may want to scoop some up each time you go in to retrieve a leg or two.

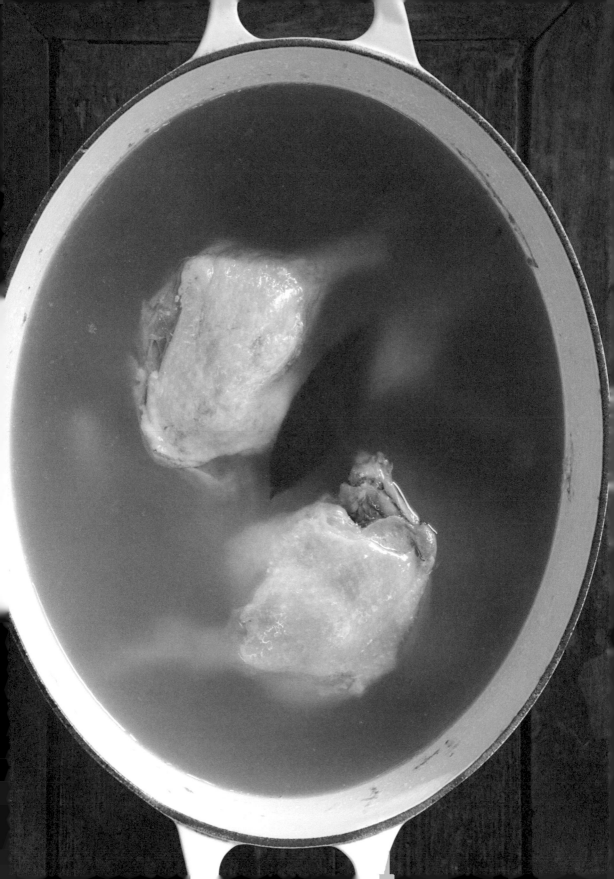

CHICKEN WITH SCALLION DUMPLINGS
serves 4

Like everyone else, we often are racing home to a house full of hollow-eyed, hungry people. We need to get something on the table quickly, and this dish can be ready in 45 minutes (that's quick to us). It's traditionally made with a whole chicken, but we use ubiquitous boneless, skinless chicken thighs because they cook quickly, and we add lean green celery and young leeks. It gives us just enough time to stand in the kitchen while dinner cooks, drink a glass of wine, nibble a piece of cheese, and talk over the day. When we serve the chicken with its pillowy dumplings, everyone agrees it was worth the wait.

FOR THE CHICKEN

3 tablespoons butter

1–2 leeks, well washed, trimmed, and sliced

5 ribs celery, chopped, leaves reserved

Handful of parsley leaves, chopped

1 clove garlic, sliced

1 pound boneless, skinless chicken thighs

Salt and pepper

1 cup chicken stock or white wine

FOR THE SCALLION DUMPLINGS

1 cup flour

1 teaspoon baking powder

½ teaspoon sugar

½ teaspoon salt

1 egg, lightly beaten

½ cup half-and-half

3–4 scallions, chopped

For the chicken, melt the butter in a heavy pot with a lid over medium heat. Add the leeks, celery, parsley, and garlic and cook until they have softened, about 10 minutes. Add the chicken and season with salt and pepper. Add the stock or wine. Cover, reduce the heat to low, and cook for 30 minutes.

Meanwhile, for the dumplings, sift or whisk together the flour, baking powder, sugar, and salt in a bowl. Stir the egg and the half-and-half into the flour. Add the scallions. The dumpling dough should be like very wet biscuit dough.

Remove the lid and using two tablespoons, drop mounds of the dumpling dough on top of the simmering chicken. You should have 8 dumplings. Cover and cook until the dumplings are cooked through, about 5 minutes.

CHICKEN THIGHS WITH LEMON

We're crazy for pan-fried chicken thighs. We cook them like we do duck breasts, putting them skin side down in the skillet over moderate heat, resisting the urge to turn them until the fat has rendered and the skin is golden brown and crisp.

Put 1 tablespoon olive oil into a large, heavy skillet over medium heat. Season 8 chicken thighs with salt and pepper and add them to the skillet skin side down. Cook them like this, without moving them, until the fat has rendered out and the skin is deep golden brown and crisp, 15–30 minutes. Fiddle with the heat, reducing it to medium-low if the skin begins to burn before it gets evenly golden brown. Turn the thighs over and stir the finely chopped rind from ½ a preserved lemon into the fat in the skillet. Continue cooking the thighs until the meat closest to the bone is cooked through, about 15 minutes more. Serve the thighs and lemony pan drippings with fat lemon wedges.—*serves 4*

CHICKEN THIGHS WITH SHERRY & MUSHROOMS: Follow the directions above for cooking the chicken thighs up to the point when you turn them over. Then add 10 ounces sliced white mushroom caps, nestling them around the thighs. Cook over medium heat until the mushrooms are tender, 15–20 minutes. Add ½ cup sherry and cook for a few minutes, then add 1 cup heavy cream. Simmer until the sauce has thickened a bit and the thighs are cooked through, 5–10 minutes. Garnish with chopped fresh chives or dill. Serve with buttered wide egg noodles, rice, or potatoes.—*serves 4*

CHICKEN THIGHS WITH BACON & OLIVES: Put 2 tablespoons olive oil and ¼ pound chopped bacon into a large, heavy skillet and cook over medium-high heat, stirring often, until the fat begins to melt into the skillet, 2–3 minutes. Add 1 sliced medium onion and 1 clove chopped garlic. Reduce heat to medium and cook, stirring often, until onions soften, 8–10 minutes. Push onions and bacon to the edge of the skillet and add 8 chicken thighs skin side down. Cook without moving them, until the fat has rendered out and the skin is deep golden brown and crisp, 15–30 minutes. Fiddle with the heat, reducing it to medium-low if the skin begins to burn before it gets evenly golden brown. Turn thighs over and add 1½–2 cups coarsely chopped pitted green olives. Spoon the onions and bacon around the thighs. Simmer until the thighs are cooked through, about 15 minutes more. Add a splash of vinegar, if you like. —*serves 4*

CHICKEN POACHED IN CREAM
serves 6

This comforting dish is a take on a childhood favorite my mother used to make with bone-in chicken breasts. The recipe she used called for Campbell's cream of celery soup. Bits of celery and onion cling to the chicken when the pieces are removed from the pot. If you want to refine this dish, brush these bits off before enrobing the poached chicken in the final velvety cream sauce. —— MH

1 chicken, 4–5 pounds
6 tablespoons butter
6 celery stalks, thinly sliced,
   leaves reserved
1 medium yellow onion, chopped

2 cups heavy cream
Salt and pepper
3 egg yolks
½ lemon

Cut the back out of the chicken (save it for making stock) and cut the chicken into 10 pieces: 4 breast pieces, 2 wings (tips removed, if you prefer), 2 drumsticks, and 2 thighs. Set aside.

Melt the butter in a heavy medium pot over medium heat. Add the celery and onions and cook, covered, until they soften, 3–5 minutes. Add the chicken, then pour in the cream. Season well with salt and pepper. Bring to a simmer. Cover the pot and reduce the heat to medium-low. Poach the chicken, turning the pieces from time to time, until the juices run clear when pierced, 45–60 minutes.

Transfer the chicken to a deep warm serving dish. Remove and discard the skin from all but the wings. Loosely cover the dish to keep the chicken warm.

Strain the cream sauce through a fine sieve into a bowl, press down on the solids, and discard them. Return the sauce to the pot. Whisk the egg yolks into the sauce and squeeze in some of the lemon juice. Simmer the sauce over medium-low heat, stirring constantly, until slightly thickened, about 5 minutes. Season with salt and pepper. Spoon the sauce over the chicken in the dish. Garnish with celery leaves. Serve with hot rice or buttered egg noodles.

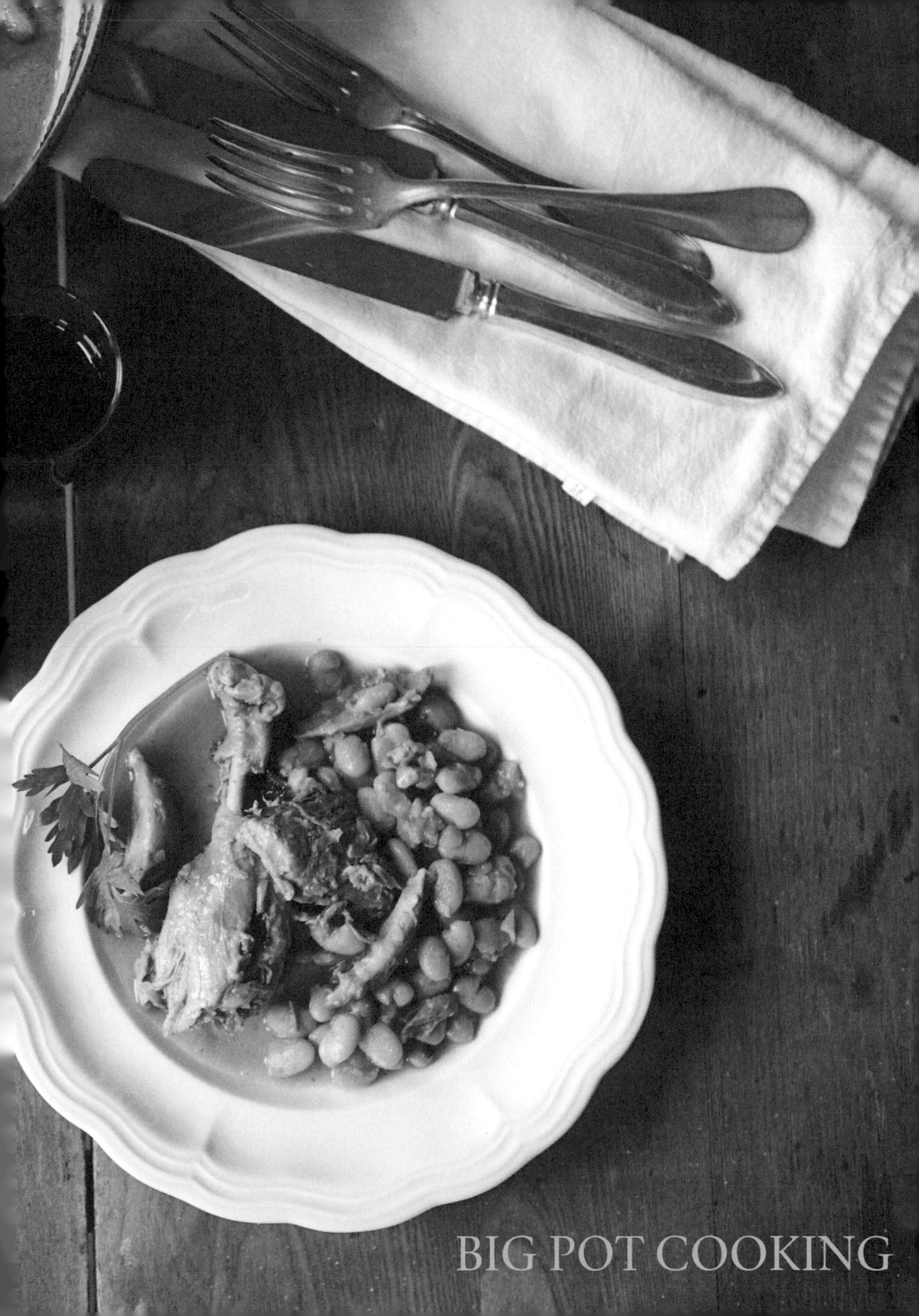

BIG POT COOKING

CASSOULET
serves 10

Give yourself a few days to prepare this classic southwest French bean dish. It's not complicated to make, but the flavors and textures need time to develop. Although we make it with what we can easily find at our local markets, we seek out the best of what's available. The dried beans we use may be tarbais one time and great Northern or navy beans another. We look for fresh garlicky pork sausages, but have used kielbasa in a pinch. Including confit of duck legs feels essential. When we don't use our own (see page 64), we buy the legs in the specialty section of the grocery store or, through mail order.

3 pounds sliced pork spareribs

2 fresh ham hocks or pork knuckles

1 raw duck carcass, completely optional

3 medium yellow onions, quartered

1 branch fresh thyme

2 bay leaves

4 ounces fatback, diced

1 smoked ham hock

2 pounds dried white beans, rinsed and picked over

8 ounces pancetta, diced

Salt and pepper

¼ cup duck fat or rendered bacon fat

1 pound fresh garlicky pork sausages, pricked

6–8 cloves garlic, minced to a paste

Confit of 6 whole duck legs (see page 64), cut at the joint into 12 pieces, legs and thighs

Put the spareribs, fresh ham hocks, duck carcass (if using), half the onions, the thyme, bay leaves, and 6 quarts (24 cups) cold water into a large heavy pot. Bring to a boil over high heat, skimming any foam that rises to the surface. Reduce the heat to medium-low and gently simmer the stock until the meats are tender, 2½–3 hours. Strain the stock into a large bowl and set aside. Retrieve the spareribs and ham hocks and set aside. Discard the remaining solids.

Put the remaining onions into a large heavy pot. Add the fat back and the smoked ham hock and cook over medium heat, stirring occasionally, until the fat has melted and the onions and smoked ham hock are lightly browned, about 10 minutes. Add the beans, pancetta, and the reserved stock and bring to a simmer over medium heat, skimming any foam. Reduce the heat to low and very gently simmer the beans until they are tender, 1½–2 hours.

Remove the pot from the heat. Season the beans with salt and pepper. Let the beans and the smoked ham hock cool in the broth.

Remove the meat from the spareribs and from both the fresh and smoked ham hocks in nice-size chunks, if possible. Set the meat aside, discarding the bones, fat, and gristle.

Melt the duck fat in a large skillet over medium heat. Add the sausages and cook until lightly browned all over, about 10 minutes. Remove the skillet from the heat and stir in the garlic.

Everything needed to assemble the cassoulet is now ready. However, it all could be covered and refrigerated overnight if you'd rather begin baking the cassoulet another day.

Preheat the oven to 325°. Using a slotted spoon, put about half of the beans and some onions, fatback, and pancetta into the bottom of a wide, deep enameled cast iron or earthenware pot. Arrange the sausages over the beans and pour the fat and garlic over them. Lay the reserved pork meat over the sausages, then arrange the duck on top. Spoon the remaining beans, onions, fatback, and pancetta over the duck. Taste the bean broth and season it with a bit more salt if it needs it, then add enough of the broth to the cassoulet to just cover the beans.

Put the cassoulet into the oven and bake for 4 hours, checking on it every hour or so to make sure it's gently bubbling along and that the beans are not drying out. When a browned skin or crust develops on the surface of the cassoulet, break it with the back of a spoon to allow moist beans to come to the surface. Add some more bean broth if the cassoulet begins to look a bit dry.

Remove the cassoulet from the oven and let it cool to room temperature. Cover it and refrigerate overnight or up to 2 days to allow the flavors to develop. Refrigerate any remaining bean broth as well.

When you are ready to finish baking the cassoulet, preheat the oven to 350°. Uncover the cassoulet and bake it for 1 hour.

Reduce the oven temperature to 300°. Break the browned crust and add enough of the reserved bean broth (or water) to just cover the beans. Bake the cassoulet for another 2 hours, adding just enough broth or water to keep the beans moist, but letting the cassoulet get browned and crusty on top. Remove the cassoulet from the oven and let it sit for 15–20 minutes, then bring it to the table to serve.

BRAISED LAMB SHANKS
serves 6

Lamb shanks need a long, gentle braise to make them utterly tender—to the point where the meat barely clings to the bone. So don't shortchange yourself of the pleasure you'll have eating this dish. Give the shanks the time they need. You'll have plenty of delicious braising liquid to serve with these shanks. Cooked white beans like gigante or baby limas, polenta, or mashed potatoes are wonderful accompaniments.

3 tablespoons olive oil

6 lamb shanks

Salt and pepper

1 small head garlic, cloves peeled

9 small yellow onions, halved lengthwise

1 cup red wine

1 cup crushed tomatoes

2 bay leaves

6–8 cups chicken stock

2 lemons, quartered

Preheat the oven to 325°. Heat the olive oil in a large, deep enameled cast iron pot over medium-high heat. Season the lamb shanks with salt and pepper. Working in batches, brown the shanks all over, about 10 minutes, transferring them to a platter as browned. Lightly brown the garlic then transfer to the platter with the shanks. Add the onions to the pot cut side down and cook without turning them until nicely browned, 3–5 minutes. Transfer them to the platter as well.

Pour off any fat and wipe out the black bits in the pot with a damp paper towel. Return the pot to medium-high heat. Add the wine and bring to a boil. Stir in the tomatoes. Return the shanks, garlic, onions, and any accumulated juices to the pot. Season with salt and pepper. Add the bay leaves and stock, then add the lemons. Cover the pot and transfer it to the oven. Braise the shanks until they are tender, about 2½ hours.

Uncover the pot and continue cooking the shanks in the oven until they are so tender the meat nearly falls off the bone and the braising juices have reduced a bit, about 1 hour.

Serve the shanks, garlic, onions, and lemon with cooked white beans, polenta, or mashed potatoes, if you like.

CHICKEN POACHED WITH HAM AND OXTAILS
serves 4–6

3 tablespoons olive oil

3 pieces oxtail

2 yellow onions, halved

Salt and pepper

2 cloves garlic

A large piece unpeeled ginger, sliced
   into rounds

½ pound boneless smoked
   pork butt

½ cup Spanish sherry

1 3–5 pound chicken

6 carrots, peeled and halved
   lengthwise

1–2 leeks, well washed, trimmed,
   and sliced

10–12 small white potatoes

Chopped fresh parsley

Heat the oil in a large, heavy pot over medium-high heat. Add the oxtail and onions. Season with salt and pepper. Sauté until they have browned on all sides, about 10 minutes. Reduce the heat to medium, add the garlic, ginger, and pork butt. Cook for 1–2 minutes then add the sherry and cook for a few more minutes. Add 8 cups water.

Put the chicken in the pot, nestling it in so that it is mostly covered by the broth. When the broth comes to a simmer, reduce the heat to low. Cover and cook for about 1 hour. Remove the chicken from the pot, and set aside until cool enough to handle. Remove all the skin and cut the chicken into pieces; legs, thighs, wings, and breast cut into 6 pieces. Cover the chicken with plastic wrap and set aside. Put the skin and any bones back into the pot. Increase the heat to medium-low and let the broth simmer and reduce for another hour.

Remove and reserve the pork butt. Strain the broth into a large bowl and discard the solids. Spoon off as much of the fat as you can, then strain the broth again back into the cleaned pot through a coffee filter or paper towel–lined strainer. It may strain slowly and you may have to change the paper towel a few times, but the resulting beautiful, clear, flavorful broth makes the effort worth it. Taste if it needs salt and pepper. Dice the pork butt and set aside.

Heat the broth over medium heat. Add the carrots, leeks, and potatoes and simmer until they are tender, about 20 minutes. Add the chicken and the diced pork butt to warm until heated through, then serve garnished with lots of chopped parsley.

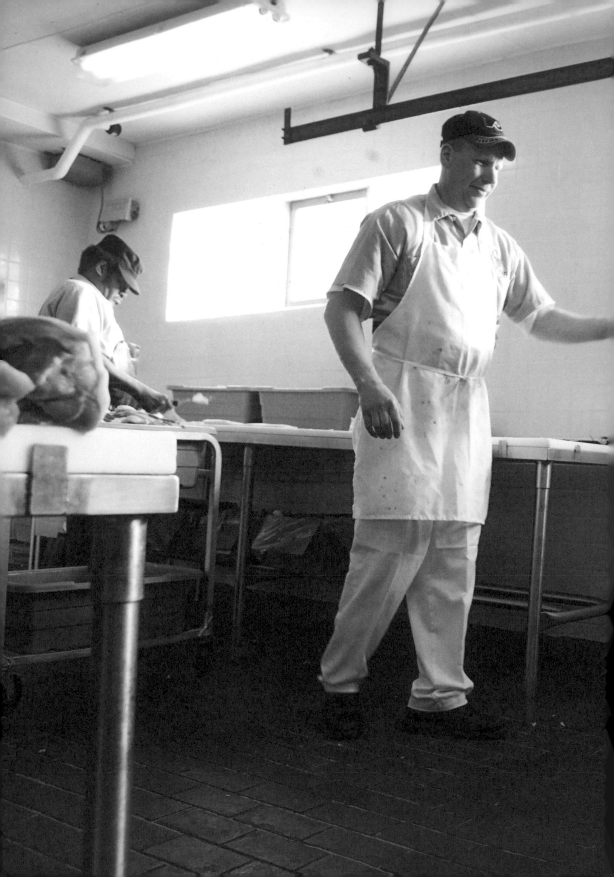

MEAT

RED STEW
serves 6–8

This is my grandmother's recipe. She named it Red Stew. Mary Gertrude, Mae to her friends, and her sister Cecelia, known as Cele, grew up Irish Catholic in San Francisco at the turn of the last century. Their family made it through the city's 1906 earthquake and fire, but the girls lost both their parents to consumption soon after. Taken in by their older sister's husband's big Italian family, they learned to straddle two cultures. Mae's stew is the perfect example. Beef and pork simmer in tomatoes and red wine with oregano and fennel seeds—Italian style. While potatoes and carrots give the stew a Gaelic flavor.

   The sisters were funny as only the Irish can be. They would watch Lawrence Welk while they sipped tiny stemmed glasses of Ficklin Port and studied the obituaries. They loved to attend wakes and funerals, but only if there was an open coffin. It was very *Arsenic and Old Lace*. As a young woman, I lived with my little daughters in the apartment across the hall from them. We ate most of our meals together—they were both terrific cooks. I learned so much of what I really know about good cooking from these two unforgettable and loving ladies. —— CH

3 tablespoons olive oil
2 yellow onions, sliced
2 cloves garlic, sliced
1 handful fresh oregano leaves, finely chopped
1 tablespoon freshly ground fennel seeds
1 teaspoon crushed red pepper flakes
Salt and pepper

2 pounds pork shoulder/butt, cut into 10 big pieces
2 pounds chuck steak, cut into 10 pieces
1 cup red wine, optional
1 28-ounce can whole tomatoes
4–6 carrots, peeled and cut into pieces
6 small boiling potatoes, peeled
Cooked polenta, optional

Preheat the oven to 325°. Heat the oil in a large, heavy pot with a lid over medium-high heat. Add the onions, garlic, oregano, fennel, and red pepper flakes. Season with salt and pepper. Cook, stirring often, until the onions have softened. Add the pork, beef, and wine if you are using it, then add the tomatoes, crushing them with your hand as you drop them into the pot, along with any juices. Bring to a simmer, then cover and cook in the oven. After about 1½ hours, add the carrots and potatoes and cook until the meat is very tender, about 3 hours total. Serve with polenta, if you like.

Overleaf: Illg's Meats, Chalfont, Pennsylvania

STUFFED FLANK STEAK
serves 4–6

This recipe is our version of the classic Argentine recipe, *matambre*, which translates loosely to "hunger killer". In South America they roll the flank steak around whole eggs and whole carrots so when you slice through the meat it presents a mosaic of beautiful colors. But it is a bit of a bear to handle, all this stuffing, and after all the work, the rolled stuffed, steak sometimes just won't hold together. So instead, we chop our stuffing into a coarse paste, spreading it on the meat so it rolls up very easily into a nice neat package. Let the meat rest before slicing so that the stuffing can reabsorb some of its juices. You can serve this hot or cold.

3 hard-boiled eggs, peeled and chopped
1 cup chopped parsley
1 cup chopped pitted green olives
½ cup fresh bread crumbs
4 anchovy fillets, minced into a rough paste

2 cloves garlic, minced
Healthy dollop of harissa
Salt and pepper
One 3-pound flank steak
Extra-virgin olive oil

Preheat the oven to 350°. Mix the eggs, parsley, olives, bread crumbs, anchovies, garlic, and harissa together in a mixing bowl. Taste the stuffing for salt. The olives and anchovies already add great flavor and saltiness, so season with salt and pepper only if needed.

Lay the flank steak flat on a cutting board. Using a large, sharp slicing or chef's knife, slice through the steak parallel to the board almost all the way through the steak. Open the steak up like a book (see photograph, pages 82 and 83). Pound the steak with a meat pounder to flatten it evenly. Spread the stuffing all over the flattened steak. Roll the steak up with the grain and tie it into a neat package with kitchen string.

Heat a splash of oil in a heavy enamel cast iron or cast iron pot over medium-high heat. Brown the meat, turning it as it cooks until it is browned all over, about 5 minutes. Transfer to the oven and cook until internal temperature reaches 125°.

Allow the roast to rest for 15–30 minutes. Remove the string before slicing into ½-inch-thick slices.

SLOW-ROASTED BONELESS PORK SHOULDER
serves 6–8

In a town nearby, there's a small country butcher shop that we've been going to for years. In the meat case you'll find tubs of marinating speedies, coiled lamb sausages, house-smoked ham hocks, whole chickens and smoked breasts, the usual cuts of beef and lamb, and, among other things, a few seasoned and trussed boneless pork shoulders ready to go straight into the oven. The seasonings vary depending on what's available or on hand—chopped parsley, thyme, sage, rosemary—but we particularly like it when they include thin slices of lemon, a nice foil for the rich pork. Ask your butcher to season and truss your pork shoulder or do it yourself as we describe below.

This roast wins the slow food cooking contest. It's amazing how tender the meat gets and how fragrant juices accumulate in the pot as it cooks. It's a beautiful thing to slip this into the oven at the beginning of the day and then pull it out perfectly cooked just in time for dinner.

I 6–7 pound boneless pork shoulder/butt

I handful fresh rosemary, parsley, or other herb leaves, finely chopped

4 cloves garlic, thinly sliced

Salt and pepper

½ lemon, thinly sliced

Lay the meat out on a clean work surface, fat side down. Season it with the chopped herbs, garlic, and plenty of salt and pepper. Arrange the slices of lemon on top. Gather the loose folds of the pork together to enclose the seasonings and make a nice neat package by trussing the roast shut with kitchen string. Rub salt and pepper all over the roast. Cover the meat and refrigerate it for a few hours, or, for more flavor, overnight.

Preheat the oven to 200°. Put the roast into an enameled cast iron pot with a tight-fitting lid. Cover the pot and slide it into the oven. Roast the pork (resisting the urge to check on it as it cooks) until it is fully tender and a lot of juices have accumulated in the pot, about 8 hours. Remove the lid and continue cooking the roast until it is golden brown on top and the juices have reduced a bit, 30–60 minutes.

Let the roast rest for 10–15 minutes before carving. Serve with the fragrant juices.

POACHED FILET OF BEEF
serves 6

This is our spring tonic. Do yourself a favor and make a good flavorful beef broth for this recipe—you'll be glad that you didn't resort to a can.

1 bunch asparagus

Salt

6 cups rich meat broth

6 small marrow bones

Six 6-ounce beef filets

1 bunch small carrots, peeled and quartered crosswise

1 cup shucked peas

1 cup peeled, shucked fava beans

Coarse sea salt and cracked pepper

1 small bunch fresh chives, finely chopped

6 slices crusty bread, toasted

Bring a small pot of water to a boil. Meanwhile, snap the asparagus in half and save the bottom halves for another use. Using a vegetable peeler, scrape the stems of the asparagus tips. Generously season the boiling water with salt then add the peeled tips and cook until tender, 3–4 minutes. Drain the asparagus and plunge them into a bowl of cold water to cool them down. Drain again and set aside.

Bring the broth to a gentle boil in a wide, heavy pot over medium heat. It's ideal to use a pot wide enough to accommodate the bones and the filets in a single layer. Place the marrow bones in the pot and poach, partially covered, until the marrow in the center softens, about 10 minutes. Turn the bones over halfway through if the broth doesn't cover them.

Tie kitchen string around each filet to make them nice and uniformly round, then set aside.

Add the carrots to the pot with the marrow bones and poach for 10 minutes. Add the beef, peas, and favas and poach until the filets are medium-rare pink in the center or have reached an internal temperature of 120°, about 10 minutes. Poach the beef a little longer if you like your meat more well done.

Heat the asparagus in the broth. Divide the marrow bones, filets, and vegetables between 6 deep, warm plates, then ladle some of the broth over all. Season with coarse salt, pepper, and sprinkle with chives. Spoon the marrow onto the toast at the table.

CORNED BEEF AND CABBAGE (and other vegetables)
serves 6–8

It wouldn't be Saint Paddy's Day without a platter of corned beef and vegetables for dinner. There's never enough leftover to make as much corned beef hash as we like the next day so we often throw two corned briskets into the pot to cook.

1 corned beef brisket (3–4 pounds), preferably the bottom round cut, rinsed

2 bay leaves

12 peppercorns

8 all-purpose white potatoes, peeled

1–2 bunches carrots, peeled

1 head savoy cabbage, cut into 8 wedges

1 handful fresh parsley leaves, chopped

1 small bunch fresh chives, minced

FOR THE HORSERADISH CREAM

2 tablespoons freshly grated, peeled horseradish or drained prepared horseradish

Juice of ½ lemon

1 cup whipped cream

1 small bunch fresh chives, minced

Salt and pepper

Put the meat, bay leaves, and peppercorns into a large, heavy pot and cover with cold water. Bring to a boil, skimming any foam. Reduce heat to maintain a gentle simmer. Partially cover the pot and simmer until the meat is very tender, about 3 hours. Transfer the meat to a platter and loosely cover with foil.

Strain the broth, returning it to the pot. Put the vegetables into the pot and gently cook over medium heat until quite tender, 30–45 minutes for the potatoes; 20–30 minutes for the carrots and cabbage. Transfer the vegetables as done to the platter with the corned beef. Reserve the cooking broth in the pot.

For the horseradish cream, fold the horseradish, lemon juice, and chives into the whipped cream in a medium bowl. Season with salt and pepper.

Reheat the corned beef in the simmering broth until warmed through. Transfer the meat to a cutting board and thinly slice. Reheat the vegetables in the broth. Reserve the cooking broth to make Corned Beef Hash with Poached Eggs (see page 91), if you like. Arrange sliced corned beef on a warm serving platter with the vegetables. Ladle some of the broth over all. Garnish with parsley and chives. Serve with the horseradish cream.

CORNED BEEF HASH WITH POACHED EGGS
serves 6

1 cooked corned beef brisket (see page 90), with cooking broth reserved

2 medium russet potatoes, peeled

2 medium yellow onions

1 small handful fresh parsley leaves, chopped

Salt and pepper

4 tablespoons butter

1 teaspoon white vinegar

6–12 eggs

Put the corned beef cooking broth into a large pot. Add the potatoes and onions and boil over medium heat until tender, about 45 minutes. Transfer to a bowl. If the onions are not tender enough, continue boiling them until they are, then add them to the bowl with the potatoes. Discard all but about ¼ cup of the cooking broth.

Use two forks to shred the corned beef into bite-size pieces, then put the shredded meat into a bowl. Coarsely chop the potatoes. Cut the onions in half, then slice them about ¼ inch thick. Add the potatoes and onions to the corned beef. Stir in the parsley and moisten it all with some of the reserved cooking broth. Taste the hash and season it with salt and pepper.

Preheat the oven to 200°. Melt 2 tablespoons of the butter in a large nonstick skillet over medium heat. Spoon half of the corned beef mixture into the skillet, shaping it into a flat cake with a metal spatula. Cook until the bottom is crisp, about 5 minutes, then flip (re-forming into a cake) and cook until crisp on the second side, about 5 minutes. Transfer the hash to a cookie sheet and keep it warm in the oven. Brown the remaining corned beef mixture in the remaining 2 tablespoons of butter in the same manner. Transfer it to the oven.

To poach the eggs, bring a deep pan of salted water to a simmer over medium heat. Add the vinegar. Crack an egg into a saucer, then gently slip it into the simmering water. Poach a few eggs at a time until the whites are opaque and the yolks are soft, about 5 minutes. Transfer the eggs with a slotted spoon to paper towels to drain.

Divide the hash between six warm plates. Season with pepper. Place 1 or 2 eggs on each portion of hash and serve.

HAM IN A POT
makes enough to feed a village for a week

When we bought a huge ham—too big to fit in our roasting pan—it was time for Plan B. We spied a blue and white speckled enamelware lobster pot high on a top shelf. It looked like a fit. We prepared the ham, then lowered it down into the pot. It cooked beautifully and it was so easy to drag around—the pot had a lid and handles. The lovely glazed ham was the centerpiece of a friend's birthday party, then back in the pot it went and was passed between four families for a week. Then the bone went into a big pot of beans. It takes a village to finish off a ham.

A bone-in ham will feed 3–4 people per pound.

1 small jar Dijon mustard
1½ cups brown sugar
1 cup real maple syrup

1 cup orange marmalade
One 20-pound bone-in smoked ham

Preheat the oven to 250°. Mix together the mustard, brown sugar, maple syrup, and orange marmalade in a mixing bowl and set aside.

Use a sharp knife to remove the rind from most of the ham, leaving a band around the end of the shank bone. Leave a thin layer of fat all over the ham and score the fat. Spread the sugar and mustard mixture over the whole ham. Put the ham in a large roasting pan or a big pot (be sure it will fit in your oven).

Bake the ham for about 6 hours, basting it every now and then. Remove from the oven and allow it to rest for 30 minutes before slicing.

SCHNITZEL AND SALAD
serves 4

We like the Milanese style of keeping the bone attached to the meat to make a pork chop into our version of schnitzel. Lean pork cuts, which can be tough and dry, turn tender when you pound them out thin and cook them quickly.

4 bone-in center loin pork chops
1 cup flour
2–3 eggs, lightly beaten
2 cups panko
12 tablespoons (1½ sticks) butter
4 tablespoons olive oil

Salt
1 recipe Mock Caesar (see page 35), romaine leaves chopped and croutons omitted
1–2 lemons, quartered

Preheat the oven to 250°. Using a meat pounder or the bottom of a small, heavy saucepan, pound the meat of each chop out between two sheets of plastic wrap on a sturdy surface to a thinness of ¼ inch or thinner without tearing the meat.

Dredge each chop in flour, then in egg, then in panko. Melt 3 tablespoons of the butter and 1 tablespoon of the oil in a large skillet over medium to medium-low heat. Fry a chop until golden brown, 5–6 minutes per side. Season with salt. Transfer the chop to a baking sheet and keep it warm in the oven. Wipe out the skillet, return it to the heat, and repeat frying the remaining chops, one at a time, in the remaining butter and oil. Keep chops warm in the oven. Serve each chop with some salad piled on top and with a wedge of lemon.

the pasta lesson

FRESH PASTA
makes enough to serve 4

Fresh homemade pasta, rolled out with a hand-cranked pasta machine, couldn't be easier. Follow our step-by-step photo guide on the preceding pages.

2 cups unbleached all-purpose flour, plus more for dusting

4 large eggs
Large pinch of salt

Put the flour into a medium mixing bowl and make a well in the center of the mound. Add the eggs and salt to the well and beat with a fork. Continue gently beating the eggs while gradually stirring in the flour, little by little, from the inside rim of the well. When the dough is too lumpy to work with the fork, use your hand and knead in the remaining flour into a ball.

Transfer the dough in the bowl to a lightly floured work surface. With clean dry hands, knead the dough, dusting it with flour as you work, until it becomes a smooth supple ball and is no longer tacky. Press your thumb into the center of the dough; if the center feels tacky, knead in a little more flour. Cover the dough with an inverted bowl or wrap it in plastic wrap and let it rest for at least 30 minutes and up to several hours.

Cut the dough into quarters and keep it covered until ready to use. Working with one piece of dough at a time, flatten the dough a bit into a rectangle then feed the narrow end through the smooth cylinders of a hand-crank pasta machine set on the widest setting. Do this two or three times to make the dough uniform. Decrease the setting on the machine by one notch and feed the narrow end of the dough through the cylinders again. Repeat this process, decreasing the setting by one notch each time. Roll the pasta as thin as you like. We find the thinness of the sheets of pasta rolled through all but the last notch the most versatile. Lay the sheet of pasta out on a lightly floured surface and cover with a clean, damp dishcloth to keep it from drying out until you're ready to cut it.

COOKED FRESH SHEETS OF PASTA

Have your filling ready to go before cooking the sheets of pasta so the pasta is nice and hot when you assemble the dish.

Bring a large pot of salted water to a boil. Cook the pasta, a few sheets at a time to keep them from sticking to each other, until tender, about 1 minute. Transfer them with a slotted spoon to a clean dishcloth (laying them out so they don't touch) and blot dry. Use the sheets of pasta as directed in the recipes below.

BUTTERNUT SQUASH & CANDIED BACON
serves 8 as a first course

1 pound slab bacon, trimmed of rind and excess layer of fat

½ cup dark brown sugar

4 cups ¼-inch-thick bite-size slices butternut squash

16 tablespoons (2 sticks) butter

1 handful fresh parsley leaves, chopped

Salt and pepper

16 sheets fresh pasta (see page 100), each 4–5 inches long, cooked

Parmigiano-reggiano

Preheat the oven to 400°. Cut the bacon into small cubes and toss with the brown sugar in a bowl. Spread the bacon out on a foil-lined baking sheet. Bake until the pieces are glazed and crisp yet meaty, about 20 minutes.

Put the squash into a large pot of salted water and gently boil over medium heat until tender, 5–10 minutes. Drain and set aside.

Melt the butter in a large skillet over medium heat. When it begins to turn golden, add the squash and cook until just warmed through. Add the parsley and season with salt and pepper.

For each serving, place a sheet of hot pasta on a warm, deep plate. Spoon some of the squash and the butter in the center of the pasta. Add a spoonful or two of the candied bacon. Drape another sheet of pasta over the filling and spoon a little more butter on top. Grate cheese over the pasta.

BROWN BUTTER & FRIED SAGE

Melt 8–12 tablespoons butter in a large skillet over medium heat. Add 20–24 fresh sage leaves and cook until the leaves are crisp and the butter has a nutty fragrance and turns golden brown (don't let it get too dark or it will taste bitter), about 2 minutes. Divide 16 sheets (each 4–5 inches long) of hot cooked pasta between 4 warm deep plates, spooning some of the sage leaves and butter between the sheets and over the pasta. Season with salt. Grate parmigiano-reggiano over the pasta.—*serves 4*

CANNELLONI
serves 4–6

Everyone in my family is crazy for this elaborate stuffed pasta dish. It is always top of the list for birthday dinners and special occasions. —— MH

FOR THE TOMATO SAUCE
One 28-ounce can crushed tomatoes
1 yellow onion, halved
4–6 tablespoons butter
Salt and pepper

FOR THE FILLING
2 tablespoons extra-virgin olive oil
1 small yellow onion, minced
1 clove garlic, minced
1 chicken liver, diced
6 ounces boneless, skinless chicken thighs, diced
6 ounces ground pork
6 ounces ground veal

Salt and pepper
Freshly grated nutmeg

FOR THE BÉCHAMEL
4 tablespoons butter
¼ cup flour
2 cups hot milk
¼ cup grated parmigiano-reggiano
Salt and pepper

TO ASSEMBLE
Salt
12 sheets Fresh Pasta (see page 100), 4 × 5 inches each
¼ cup grated parmigiano-reggiano
2–3 tablespoons butter

For the tomato sauce, put the crushed tomatoes into a medium saucepan. Rinse the can with a little water to get the remaining tomatoes out and pour the liquid into the saucepan. Add the onions and butter and season with salt and pepper. Simmer over medium-low heat, stirring occasionally, until the onions soften and the sauce thickens a bit, about 30 minutes.

Taste the sauce. Depending on the canned tomatoes you've used, you may want to soften the sauce's acidity with a little more butter, the more butter the softer and rounder the flavors. On occasion, we've had to add a pinch or two of sugar to balance the acidity. Remove and discard the onions from the sauce before using.

For the filling, heat the oil in a large skillet over medium heat. Add the onions and garlic and cook until soft, 3–5 minutes. Add the chicken livers, if using, and cook until they are no longer pink. Add the chicken, pork, and veal and season well with salt and pepper. Cook the meat, breaking it up with a fork or the back of a spoon, until it is cooked through and much of the liquid has evaporated, about 10 minutes.

Working in batches, transfer the meat to a cutting board and chop it until its texture is quite fine, like a coarse paste. Or, pulse the meat in a food processor until it just begins to hold together, but avoid turning the meat into a smooth paste! Season the filling with a couple pinches nutmeg and a little more salt and pepper if it needs it. Transfer to a mixing bowl and set aside.

For the béchamel, melt the butter in a medium saucepan over medium-low heat. Sift in the flour and cook, stirring constantly, until the flour loses its raw taste yet has not taken on any color (it should remain white), 1–2 minutes. Gradually whisk in the milk then stir constantly until the sauce is as thick as heavy cream, about 10 minutes.

Remove the pan from the heat and stir in the cheese. Season with salt and pepper. Add about ½ cup of the béchamel to the meat filling. Cover the surface of the remaining béchamel with a sheet of plastic wrap to prevent a skin from forming and set aside in a warm spot.

Bring a large pot of salted water to a boil. Cook 2–3 sheets of pasta at a time until tender, about 30 seconds, then transfer them with a slotted spoon to a large bowl of cold water to cool. Lay the sheets of cooked pasta out on clean damp kitchen towels in a single layer without touching. Cover with more damp towels.

To assemble the cannelloni, spread 2–3 tablespoons of the meat filling along the wide edge of a sheet of pasta, then roll it up jelly roll style. Repeat with the remaining filling and sheets of pasta.

Spread about half of the tomato sauce over the bottom of a large baking dish. Nestle the cannelloni, overlapping side down, into the dish in a single layer. Spread the remaining tomato sauce over the cannelloni. Spoon the reserved béchamel over the sauce, making a swath down the center of the dish. Sprinkle the top with the cheese and dot with small knobs of the butter. The prepared cannelloni can keep up to this point in the refrigerator, covered with plastic wrap, for up to 2 days, or in the freezer for up to 2 weeks. (It does not need to be defrosted before going into the oven to bake.)

Preheat the oven to 375°. Bake the cannelloni until the sauce is bubbling hot and the top is lightly browned in spots, 15–30 minutes.

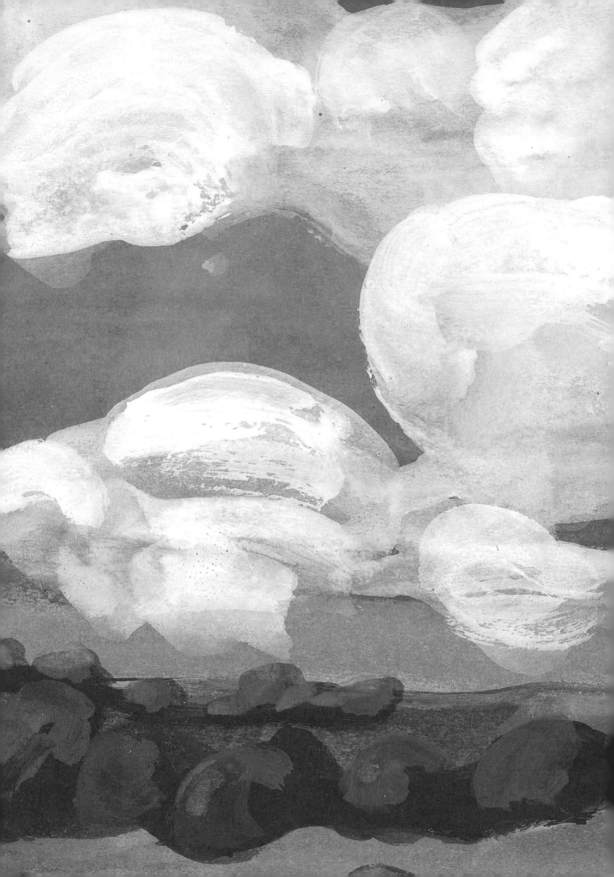

easter lunch

PASTA PRIMAVERA
serves 8

A few years back, pasta primavera used to turn up on every salad bar, no matter the season. Seems to us pasta primavera should be made in the spring (thus the name) with just the first young vegetables. If you look up the recipe on the Internet—tempting and convenient but not always with the best re-sults—you'll find versions made with carrots, cherry tomatoes, bell peppers, *herbes de Provence* and rotelli. We prefer little favas, peas, and asparagus, all tangled up in a few strands of spaghetti.

Salt
2 tablespoons extra-virgin olive oil
1 cup diced smoked ham
1 cup fava beans, blanched and peeled
1 cup shucked fresh or frozen
  English peas
1½ cups chopped thin asparagus

Pepper
1 pound spaghetti
1 tablespoon tomato paste
Really good extra-virgin olive oil
Finely chopped fresh mint leaves
Grated pecorino romano

Fill a large pot with water, add a few pinches of salt, and bring the water to a boil over medium heat.

Meanwhile heat the olive oil in a large skillet over medium heat. Add the ham, and cook, stirring often, until the ham is lightly browned. Add the favas, peas, and asparagus, season with salt and pepper, then add a splash of water. Cook, stirring often, until the vegetables are just cooked, about 3 minutes. Remove from the heat, cover, and set aside.

Add the pasta to the boiling water and cook until just tender, about 10 min-utes. Drain, return it to the pot, add the tomato paste, drizzle with some really good extra-virgin olive oil, and season with salt and pepper.

Add the ham and vegetables and all their pan juices to the pasta and gently toss everything together. Divide between 8 individual warm bowls and sprinkle with fresh mint and pecorino romano.

ROAST LEG OF LAMB IN THE OVEN
serves 8–10

Lamb. And spring. They are inextricable. We roast a leg for Easter, or a whole animal outside on a spit over an applewood fire. We are eager to be out again after the long cold winter and it's just warm enough to do so. But the weather toys with us, throwing us bone-chilling rain, even furious snow flurries. Undaunted, we just step closer to the fire to keep warm. The more smoke, the more perfumed the lamb.

One early spring afternoon we gathered friends together for a feast in honor of our friend Peggy Knickerbocker, who was visiting from the West Coast. We spit-roasted a whole lamb in the back yard. It was 25 pounds, and we were anxious that the young lamb wouldn't yield enough meat for the gathering. We ran out and bought an extra leg, then roasted it in front of the fireplace in the living room, suspended from a string attached to a nail that was driven into the mantel. The roast spun around on its string, winding up and winding down in perpetual motion. Richard Olney wrote about this way of roasting lamb in *Lulu's Provençal Table* (Ten Speed Press, 2002)—and it works beautifully. The lamb was plentiful and most delicious that day. The spit-roast was distinctively smoky and almost wild tasting as it always is when cooked outside; the other was meaty and perfectly rosy throughout.

The preparation of the meat is the same for either way you choose to roast your lamb. We order it semiboneless from the butcher—the tail, pelvic, and thigh bones removed, leaving the shank bone intact. This gives the lamb a "handle" or something nice to hold when you're carving beautiful slices of meat, and you don't have to maneuver around the bones.

One 8–10 pound leg of lamb, tail, pelvic, and thigh bones removed; shank bone and heel left attached
4 cloves garlic, minced
4 anchovy fillets, minced
1 bunch fresh parsley, leaves chopped
Salt and pepper
Really good extra-virgin olive oil
1 handful fresh rosemary leaves
4–5 lemons, halved

Put the leg of lamb on a clean work surface and open up the meat so it lays out flat. Make a paste with the garlic, anchovies, half the parsley, and some salt and pepper, then rub it into the meat. Gather the loose folds of meat together to enclose the seasonings and make a nice neat package by trussing the roast shut with kitchen string. Put the lamb into a large dish. Rub about 2 tablespoons olive oil, the rosemary, and a generous seasoning of salt and pepper all over the roast. Let the lamb rest like this for a few hours, at room temperature, or refrigerate it overnight. (Let the lamb return to room temperature before roasting it.)

Preheat the oven to 350°. Put the seasoned leg of lamb into a heavy roasting pan, meatier side up. Roast the lamb until it is browned and crusty and the meat inside is rosy with an internal temperature in the thickest part registering 120° for rare, about 45 minutes; 130° for medium-rare, about 1 hour; and 150° for medium, about 1½ hours. Transfer the lamb to a warm serving platter or a cutting board, cover it loosely with foil, and let it rest for 10–20 minutes before carving. Skim off the fat from the pan juices.

Carve the lamb and serve it garnished with the remaining chopped parsley and the lemons. Pass the meat juices at the table.

LEG OF LAMB ROASTED IN FRONT OF THE FIRE: Prepare a hot fire in your fireplace. Mix together ¼ cup olive oil, juice of ½ lemon, and salt and pepper to taste in a small bowl and set aside.

When the fire is hot and there is a good bed of coals, tie a sturdy piece of kitchen string around the shank bone above the heel of the seasoned, trussed leg of lamb (see previous recipe) and tie the other end to a hook or sturdy nail in the face of the mantel so that the leg of lamb hangs directly in front of the hot fire and is suspended about 6-inches or so above a wide pan placed on the hearth floor to collect any drippings as the lamb roasts. The leg will begin rotating on its own. Give it a gentle twist in the direction it is already turning. The lamb will now have enough momentum to gently rotate back and forth.

Brush the lamb with the seasoned oil every 15 minutes or so and give the heel a little twist whenever the roast needs it to keep the gentle rotating motion going. Add more wood to the fireplace to maintain a good hot fire. Cook the lamb in this fashion until it is browned and rosy on the inside with an internal temperature registering 130° for medium-rare, about 1½ hours. Transfer the lamb to a warm serving platter or a cutting board, cover it loosely with foil, and let it rest for 10–20 minutes before carving. Carve the lamb and serve it garnished with chopped parsley and lemons.—*serves 8–10*

ARTICHOKES ROMAN STYLE
serves 5–10

Roman artichokes are prized for their tenderness. While California arties are delicious, you have to peel off the outer leaves get to the pale green inner ones that are tender enough to eat. Most self-respecting Romans might turn up their beautiful Roman noses at our thistly orbs. But this is what we find in the market, so we prepare them as they do in the Eternal City, with olive oil and wine and fresh mint—and they are transformed.

I large bunch mint, trimmed of
  stems and minced (about I cup)
2 cloves garlic, minced
I cup olive oil, plus a splash

5 large artichokes
I lemon, halved
I bottle dry white wine
Salt and pepper

Mix together the mint and garlic in a mixing bowl and add a splash of olive oil.

Pull off and discard all the tough outer leaves of the artichokes (snapping off the leaves just before the bottom to leave behind the meat at the bottom of the leaf) until you get to the tender pale green inner leaves. Slice off about 2-inches from the top. Peel, then cut stems to 1 inch. Use a sharp paring knife to trim away and smooth the stems and bottoms. As you trim, rub the flesh with the cut lemon to prevent the artichoke from turning brown.

Spread the leaves apart and use a melon baller or small sharp spoon to scoop out and discard the hairy choke. Pack inside the artichoke and between the leaves with the mint and garlic.

Arrange the artichokes stems up in a large heavy nonreactive pot (not aluminum or cast iron). Pour the oil over the artichokes then pour in the wine. Season with salt and pepper. Cover and cook over medium heat until the artichokes are very tender when pierced with a knife.

Transfer the artichokes to a platter, set aside, and allow to cool. Increase the heat to medium-high and reduce the wine and oil by half. Meanwhile, when cool enough to handle, cut the artichokes in half lengthwise or leave them whole if you prefer. Spoon the sauce over them and serve.

A BIG MERINGUE WITH "EXOTIC" FRUITS
serves 8–12

Easter dessert. You want to serve something as pretty and showy as an Easter bonnet. The holiday usually comes too early in the spring for any of the delicious local fruits, so we like to serve this big meringue piled high with billowy whipped cream, decorated with sweet, tart "exotic" fruits or fresh strawberries if they are in season in your neck of the woods.

4 large egg whites, at room temperature
Pinch of cream of tartar
1 cup superfine sugar
1 teaspoon white vinegar
½ teaspoon vanilla extract

1½ cups heavy cream
Exotic fruits: 1 ripe pineapple, peeled, cored, and cut into chunks; 2–3 bananas, peeled and sliced; 4 kiwi, peeled, quartered, and sliced; pulp of 2 passion fruits

Preheat the oven to 275°. Line a cookie sheet with parchment paper and set aside.

Put the egg whites and cream of tartar into a large mixing bowl. Beat the whites on medium speed until they are very foamy, then increase the speed to medium-high and beat until they hold medium-stiff peaks. Continue beating on medium-high speed and gradually add the sugar, beating in 1 tablespoon at a time. Increase the speed to high and beat the whites until they are thick, stiff, and glossy. The total beating time depends on the freshness of the egg whites and the power of your electric mixer and we've found it can take about 5 minutes and sometimes up to 10 minutes. Fold the vinegar and vanilla into the whites.

Pile the meringue into the center of the parchment paper and gently smooth it out to form a thick 9-inch circle. Put the meringue into the oven and bake for 1 hour.

Turn off the oven and leave the meringue inside to dry out and cool completely, 2–3 hours. The longer the meringue dries out the chewier and crunchier it becomes so leaving it in the turned-off oven as long as overnight is fine, too.

The meringue will have cracks around the center and sides. Peel off the parchment paper and put the meringue on a cake plate.

Just before serving, whip the cream in a mixing bowl until big soft peaks form, then pile it on top of the meringue. Arrange the fruit on top of the whipped cream and spoon the passion fruit pulp over the fruit.

something sweet

ROASTED RHUBARB

Rhubarb is one of the first plants to poke their heads through the early spring soil. Its tart flavor is refreshingly delicious. Spoon it over thick yogurt, ice cream, pound cake, or just enjoy it on its own.

Preheat the oven to 350°. Thickly slice 2 pounds rhubarb and put it into a deep oven-proof pot. Add ½ cup sugar and ½ cup red wine. Split open 1 or 2 vanilla beans and add them to the rhubarb. Roast the rhubarb until very tender, about 30 minutes.—*makes 2–3 cups*

LIME CURD TART
makes one 9- or 10-inch tart

It's the buttery short crust against the tangy lime curd filling that makes this tart so delicious. Choose fat, smooth-surfaced, thin-skinned limes—they tend to be juicier than the thick-skinned variety. During the winter months, when Meyer lemons are in season, we sometimes substitute them for the limes to make a sweet-tart tart. This tart is a version of a recipe I found in *Food & Wine* magazine more than twenty years ago. —— MH

FOR THE CRUST
1½ cups flour
¾ cup powdered sugar, sifted
Pinch of salt
10 tablespoons cold unsalted butter,
  cut into small pieces

FOR THE FILLING
2 whole eggs
4 egg yolks
4–6 limes, depending on their juiciness
1½ cups granulated sugar
6 tablespoons unsalted butter, cut
  into small pieces

Freshly whipped cream

For the crust, whisk the flour, powdered sugar, and salt together in a medium mixing bowl. Using your fingers, work the butter into the flour, then rub the flour and butter together until the dough forms a smooth ball. Shape the dough into a disk. Press the dough evenly into and up the sides of a 9- to 10-inch round false-bottom fluted tart pan. The dough should be about ¼ inch thick. Trim off any excess dough. Prick the crust all over with the tines of a fork. Cover the crust with plastic wrap and refrigerate for at least an hour, or overnight.

continued

Preheat the oven to 350°. Set the tart pan on a baking sheet and bake the crust until it is golden, 20–30 minutes. The crust will slouch down from the top of the tart pan rim a bit, but that's okay. Set the crust aside to cool completely.

For the filling, gently whisk together the eggs and the yolks in a medium bowl and set aside. Wash the limes in warm water and pat them dry. Finely grate the zest of 4 of the limes into a medium nonreactive saucepan. Juice the limes to make about ⅔ cup of juice; if the limes are juicy and you end up with a little more juice, use it. Add the juice to the saucepan and whisk in the granulated sugar.

Set the saucepan over medium-low heat and whisk in the eggs. Cook the filling, whisking constantly to prevent it from boiling, until it has thickened, 5–8 minutes.

Remove the saucepan from the heat and add the butter, a few knobs at a time, whisking until the butter has melted. Strain the lime curd filling through a sieve into a medium bowl. Cover the surface with plastic wrap or parchment paper to prevent a skin from forming. Set it aside to cool.

Spoon the filling into the prepared tart crust and smooth out the top with a rubber spatula. Refrigerate the tart for at least an hour and up to 8 hours so that the filling can set. Serve the tart with big dollops of whipped cream.

DRIED APRICOT TART
makes one 12-inch tart

This recipe, from a friend who urged us to try it, has become a winter favorite. An almond cream envelopes the white wine-plumped dried apricots—delicious!

FOR THE APRICOTS
2 cups white wine
⅔ cup granulated sugar
1 cinnamon stick
Wide strips of zest from 1 lemon
1 tablespoon fresh lemon juice
1¾ cups dried apricots

FOR THE CRUST
2 cups flour
2 tablespoons granulated sugar

12 tablespoons (1½ sticks) cold
    unsalted butter, cut into pieces
1 egg

FOR THE ALMOND CREAM FILLING
¾ cup blanched almonds
¾ cup powdered sugar
2 tablespoons flour
8 tablespoons butter, cut into pieces
1 whole egg
1 egg yolk
2 teaspoons vanilla extract

continued

For the apricots, put the wine, granulated sugar, cinnamon stick, and lemon zest and juice into a medium saucepan. Bring to a gentle boil over medium heat, stirring until the sugar dissolves. Reduce the heat to medium-low, add the apricots to the syrup, cover, and simmer until they are plump, about 15 minutes. Remove the pan from the heat and the lid from the pan. Let the apricots cool in the syrup. (The apricots will keep in the syrup in the refrigerator for up to 1 week.) Drain the apricots, reserving the syrup for another use. Discard the cinnamon stick and lemon zest.

For the crust, whisk the flour and granulated sugar together in a large mixing bowl. Using two butter knives or your fingers, work the butter into the flour until it is crumbly and has the texture of cornmeal. Add the egg and stir with a fork until the dough begins to mass together, then press the dough together to form a smooth ball. Shape the dough into a disk. Press the dough evenly into and up the sides of a 12-inch round false-bottom fluted tart pan. The dough should be about ¼ inch thick. Trim off any excess dough. Cover the crust with plastic wrap and refrigerate for at least an hour, or overnight.

For the almond cream filling, finely grind the almonds in a food processor or nut grinder. Gently toast the ground almonds in a small skillet over medium heat, stirring almost constantly to prevent them from burning, until they are fragrant and golden, about 5 minutes. Remove the skillet from the heat and stir in the powdered sugar and flour. Set aside to cool.

Return the cooled almond mixture to the food processor. Add the butter, whole egg, egg yolk, and vanilla and process until the filling is smooth.

Preheat the oven to 400°. Using a rubber spatula, evenly spread the filling in the prepared crust. Arrange the apricots on top, gently pushing them into the filling. Bake the tart until the filling swells up around the apricots and is deep golden brown, about 45 minutes. Serve the tart just barely warm (it sets up as it cools) or at room temperature.

OUR BOOKS

This is the third book of our recipe collections—Canal House Cooking. We'll publish three seasonal volumes a year: Summer, Fall & Holiday, and Winter & Spring, each filled with delicious recipes for you from us. To sign up for a subscription or to buy books, visit thecanalhouse.com.

OUR WEBSITE

Our website, thecanalhouse.com, a companion to this book, offers our readers ways to get the best from supermarkets (what and how to buy, how to store it, cook it, and serve it). We'll tell you why a certain cut of meat works for a particular recipe, which boxes, cans, bottles, or tins are worthwhile, which apples are best for baking, and what to look for when buying olive oil, salt, or butter. We'll also suggest what's worth seeking out from specialty stores or mail-order sources and why. And wait, there's more. We will share our stories, the wines we are drinking, gardening tips, events—and our favorite books, cooks, and restaurants will all be on our site.